Romancing
the Stove

Romancing the Stove

≋

Amy Reiley

life of reiley

ISBN: 978-0-9846898-0-4

art director and designer: Deborah Daly
editor: Ronie Reiley
copy editor: Mark Siagh
editorial assistant: Sarah Goss
illustrations: Kersti Frigell
front cover photography: Lisa Peju
test kitchen directors: Delahna Flagg; Brooke Newberry
contributing chefs: James Boyce; Tina Casaceli; Amelia Ceja; Jack Czarnecki; Brad Farmerie; Susan Feniger; Bradford Kent; Pat Rabin; Philippe Rispoli; Annette Tomei; Chrysta Wilson
recipe testers: Larisa A. Buch; Carol Stager Commons; Debbie Dillard; Arlene Goss; Ngoc Hoang; Rita & Mike Kassak; Laura & Jason Malartsik; Jenifer Marom; Kellee Mendoza; Marie Mercier; Rich Pedine; Paula Peterson; Jessica Rabbiner; Kendra Schussel; Jill Sazama; Nancy Siegel; Shane Soldinger; Nicolette Teo

special thanks: Sarah Casriel; Seth Casriel; Eva Crawford; Angela Dimino; Galit Hadari; Herta Peju; Lisa Peju; Courtney Pisarik; Vik Sehadri; Kelli Stember; Annette Tomei; Richard T. Williams; Arlene Winnick and Big the Chihuahua for his undying enthusiasm in cleaning up test kitchen disasters

For more on the contributing chefs, upcoming events and other additional information, visit www.romancingthestovecookbook.com

Published by Life of Reiley, www.lifeofreiley.com

PRINTED IN THE UNITED STATES OF AMERICA

Contents

ROMANCING THE STOVE

Introduction

The question I'm most often asked is, "Do aphrodisiac foods really work?"

In reply, I like to tell the story of Mr. Takeout: When I was working on my first book, *Fork Me, Spoon Me: the sensual cookbook* there was this guy. He was a friend of mine; let's call him Mr. Takeout. As the name implies, Mr. Takeout's idea of getting dinner was dialing. So, since I was generating enough food for a small army each day refining the book's recipes, I would invite Mr. Takeout over for the leftovers. I thought he was a nice guy but I never allowed my impression of him to evolve beyond that. It honestly never crossed my mind that I was feeding this man aphrodisiacs—and eating them along with him—day after day for an extended period of time. I never gave it a conscious thought, that is, until several years later on the day Mr. Takeout proposed. That was the moment when I realized that I had, inadvertently, generated what I feel is indisputable evidence that aphrodisiacs do, indeed work. Thank you, Mr. Takeout.

The Mr. Takeout experience has led, in a large part, to the evolution of my perspective on aphrodisiac foods since I wrote *Fork Me*. But it's not just my personal experiences that influenced where I wanted to go with *Fork Me*'s sequel.

It's also the stories of my friends and the strangers I come in contact with as a food writer that have shaped my perspective and influenced this book's message. There are the ones who've been over-stimulated by food television. They're the types who feel like they aren't qualified to enter their own kitchen because they haven't taken a knife skills class and ask me exactly which garlic press they should buy. (For the record, I don't own a garlic press—just a great knife.) There are the ones who make poor food choices because they don't take the time or simply haven't acquired the knowledge to feed themselves what the human body actually craves. They're the ones who don't like the way they feel or look and sense that its related to diet but aren't sure how to change. Lastly, and definitely pro-

foundly, it's the stories of the people who, for one reason or another, have developed a complete hatred for their stove. The stay-at-home parents with finicky kids who feel duty bound to produce gastronomic miracles the whole family will eat night after night; the overworked professionals who spend more hours at the office than in their homes; and ever other manner of former food enthusiast who has fallen out of love with the kitchen that inspires me to serve up romance for the libido, heart and soul.

That's why *Romancing the Stove* is all about exploring the definition of aphrodisiac foods and the many ways in which I believe aphrodisiacs can be applied not only to moments of seduction but to enhance every day. What I'm using this book to illustrate is that a much more healthy, fulfilling and, frankly, exciting relationship with aphrodisiacs is about loving food, loving cooking. It's about loving serving both delicious and wholesome food to the ones you love, as well as using food in finding and maintaining romance. The older I get, the more I understand how important it is to do things for your body to keep yourself feeling and looking good—don't we all want to wake up feeling not only our best physically but embracing our most sensual selves? To get on that path, I think you have to start with seducing yourself with the very best food choices.

With this book I want to illustrate the powers of not only many natural, aphrodisiac ingredients but also the powers of many of the nutrients found in these foods and to illustrate how they can impact libido. With the recipes, I am striving to offer ingredients and flavors

11   *Introduction*

that are not only exciting to the senses but also great for the body, packed with nutrients that will support sex drive and also influence overall health. Because believe me, I've learned that feeling sexy, looking your best and boosting your energy can be just as important in the bedroom as all those little hormones.

Food and the Art of Sensuality

I can easily feed you the history of an ingredient as an aphrodisiac or the nutrition of certain foods and how it affects your hormones or brain chemistry. And I can give you chapter upon chapter of foods to help improve your sexual hormone levels, boost your energy and get your body looking its most sexy. The fact of the matter is, yes, all of these things will help. But if you can't slow down long enough to be fully present in a romantic moment, all the aphrodisiacs in the world

aren't going to help. (Trust me, I know. I know from personal experience, I hear it from friends and, when you're known as an expert on aphrodisiac foods, perfect strangers regularly over-share.)

As our world becomes increasingly "turned on," our bodies sometimes completely shut off. (And here I mean turned on in the technological sense, although the longer you stick with the recipes and principles in this book, the more I think you'll find it getting turned on in far more rewarding ways!)

A few years ago, when I was on a trip to New York City to promote *Fork Me* on one of the national morning shows, my friend Annette (whose Thai-inspired watermelon salad recipe I've included in this book), took me on a mini tour of her colleague Brad Farmerie's two restaurants. She thought I'd enjoy seeing the direction in which Chef Farmerie, who at the time was starting to get some pretty big buzz in the culinary world, was taking his cuisine. The two meals were a revelation. All of the ingredients were familiar to me, as were the cooking techniques. But it was the way in which he layered multiple textures, flavors and temperatures into every bite of every dish that is what made probably the single greatest impression on me in recent memory.

I don't think I've ever been so completely drawn in by a meal as I was by the array of sensory pleasures this chef had packed into a single spoonful. Distractions of other diners, wait staff, cell phones, traffic—all of it ceased to exist. Suddenly it was just Annette, me and the shared experience of our dinner.

So, inspired by this life—or at least career—altering experience, I've tried to help others combat the madness of the modern age by incorporating these kind of elements into my recipes. My hope is to help other diners become more present in the moment of their meal—and whatever might follow! I find that incorporating a variety of temperatures, textures and colors (and sometimes even aromas) into a dish increases the sensuality of the dining experience by challenging the senses in a somewhat unexpected way.

Something for Every Taste, Situation and Level of (Cooking) Experience

To optimize the book's usefulness, I've divided the recipes into chapters based on their amorous effects. The first recipe chapter, Chapter 2, is designed for seduction, filled with ingredients that are known to have an immediate effect. Chapter 3 is dedicated to ingredients scientifically proven to help maintain a healthy libido. Chapter 4 is filled with indulgent dishes designed to pamper. Chapter 5 focuses on lower-calorie, nutrient-rich foods—the kinds of things you want to eat right to feel like you can throw off all your clothes without a care in the world. Another, Chapter 6, is full of quick little zingers to help you eat well even when you're short on time. Lastly, Chapter 7 is a section of snacks, because no day is complete without a little love bite.

The recipes in the book are friendly to almost any diet. There's a heavy emphasis on seafoods, known in Greek folklore as the playthings of Aphrodite but also acknowledged by modern science as packed with nutrients important to a thriving libido. Nearly half the book's recipes are vegetarian (some even vegan), which I've noted in the introduction of the vegetarian-friendly dishes. There are still plenty of options to appeal to meat lovers. But I'm a firm believer that a delicious diet doesn't need to always feature meat. Instead of centering the meals around animal protein, I'm offering a wide variety of dishes focused on freshness, vibrancy and aphrodisiac impact. Unless otherwise noted, the recipes in this book are designed for two but make four servings because I think leftovers can be supremely sexy. Just imagine packing a little lunch for your lover of the leftovers from a memorable date night. Remember that our emotions are very easily triggered by the senses. I've found that a simple whiff of the scent of

leftovers can reignite the passion the dish sparked when it was first served. And I know that sometimes, after a rather successful roll in the hay you find yourself famished. Tucking in to second helpings of your dinner is much better for the body than a late night pizza delivery (and so much more memorable than going to bed hungry!).

Because I want you to love the experience of cooking from this book, I've tried to keep my ingredient lists and instructions fairly simple, making romance accessible to every level of cook. But as I did with *Fork Me, Spoon Me,* to feed the souls of experienced cooks, I've incorporated a few recipes from noted chefs whose cuisine truly lends itself to a romantic experience. Many of these recipes are a little more challenging and incorporate exotic ingredients. But challenges can be an exhilarating part of life, bringing deliciously unexpected rewards.

~1~
What is an Aphrodisiac Food?

It's incredibly sad to me (sad is probably not a strong enough word) that the most widely known definition of an aphrodisiac food in the United States—possibly the world—is that of the American Food and Drug Administration. The FDA defines an aphrodisiac as a food that directly raises sexual hormone levels. Now, unfortunately, the government maintains that there is no evidence of any one ingredient having this kind of impact on the body. In other words, it's the FDA's stance that no food should be promoted as an aid to the world of romance.

I, obviously, have a very different definition of aphrodisiacs. After all, despite the FDA's cold shoulder toward the world's most "exciting" foods, people around the globe have throughout history, and continue to this day, considered sensual foods as aphrodisiac.

Originally, it was a fascination with this disparity between the definition of the American government and the behavior of people the world over that drew me to the topic of aphrodisiacs. I couldn't get past the fact that so many cultures—since the beginning of recorded time—held foods in regard as aphrodisiacs. Cultures on opposite sides of the world at a time before communication between the East and the West were using the same ingredients for the very same romance-related purposes, ranging from seduction to treating impotence, improving fertility, celebrating newlyweds and lifting libido. How could so many differing people come to the same conclusion if aphrodisiacs have, as the FDA states, no impact on the body?

Over the years of studying how different cultures have applied aphrodisiacs, as well as recent scientific discoveries on the topic, reflecting on personal experience and, of course, reading *Cosmo,* I started developing a theory of my own on the use, or as I see it, many uses, of aphrodisiacs.

Then one night not long ago when I was suffering a bout of insomnia, I thought I'd try lulling myself to sleep with a few chapters of Dr. Michael R. Liebowitz's *The Chemistry of Love.* (Not to say that it isn't a brilliant book but it is a far drier read than my usual bedtime chick lit—perfect insomnia fare, I figured.) But instead of being lulled back to dreamland, I was supercharged with adrenalin, energized by Dr. Liebowitz's findings, which helped to corroborate my theories on what defines an aphrodisiac food.

From the book I learned that, in the brain, we have two distinct chemical systems for romance. The first is attraction, which revs up energy and sharpens the senses. The second is attachment, in which the brain's priority is security in a relationship over excitement. Dr. Liebowitz also finds that there are special moments in every relationship that don't fit into either of these two stages of romance. These he calls "peak love experiences," to describe those almost magical moments in which our love or passion is at its most intense—those moments we try over and over again to recreate.

Now, I'll admit that there hasn't really been any serious research to demonstrate that the use of foods can assist the brain in making these changes in chemistry. However, I believe that certain applications of aphrodisiacs can be helpful in setting the stage for attraction—and maybe even make the experience of initial attraction that much more fun!

I also believe that food can be used to help us achieve those elusive "peak love experiences," not to mention offering some support in maintaining the delicate balance of that phase Dr. Liebowitz calls attachment (and most of us call marriage). In fact, without even hearing this scientific breakdown, I'd been speaking and writing on my theory that different aphrodisiac

What is an Aphrodisiac Food?

ingredients should be called upon at different stages of romance. Long before *The Chemistry of Love* epiphany, it was how I'd intended to divide the recipe chapters of my next (this) book!

Here's what I mean: some foods earn their aphrodisiac reputation for their ability to produce an immediate physiological effect on the body (useful in the attraction stage, right?). For instance, chile peppers have been used as aphrodisiacs throughout the Americas and Asia for centuries for their ability to raise body temperature and bring a blush to the cheeks similar to a sexual flush. Ginger, another warming spice, can make the eater's tongue tingle with anticipation and lips plump to a sexy pout without the need for collagen—if only temporarily. Others, like coffee, elevate mood and improve energy or, like Champagne, deliver a quick shot of giddy pleasure. These are the kinds of foods I've featured in Chapter 2, *Recipes for Seduction*.

One of the very first things I learned about aphrodisiacs, beyond their fascinating folkloric history, is that the mere scents of some foods can evoke the primal urges. Its a bit crazy to imagine a scientist dreaming up such a clinical investigation but in the late 1990s, Dr. Alan Hirsch of the Smell and Taste Treatment and Research Foundation in Chicago completed a study in which food aromas caused sexual arousal in subjects in both waking and sleeping states.

The most successful scent tested in the study to tempt men was a combination of pumpkin pie spice and lavender. (Who would have ever thought of putting them together?) For women, it was combining cucumbers with—oddly enough—black licorice candies. Other scents, such as glazed donut, buttered popcorn and vanilla showed promising results in both sexes.

I've slipped ingredients with seductive aromas into recipes throughout the book for an added layer of romance. In addition to the research of Dr. Hirsch, I've incorporated that of Dr. Max Lake, a brilliant MD, not to mention vintner, from Australia's Hunter Valley. Dr. Lake discovered similarities between the scents of certain foods and the aromas of human pheromones. I've added more in-depth discussion of Dr. Lake's work in Chapter 8, *Don't Whine—Wine!*

Continuing to absorb the findings in *The Chemistry of Love,* I became particularly fascinated with Dr. Liebowtz's discussion of romance's attachment phase. I believe that aphrodisiacs are much more important to those already in a relationship than those falling in

What is an Aphrodisiac Food?

love, that's why I've given the subject two recipe chapters: Chapter 3, *Feed Your Libido* and Chapter 4, *Unleashing Your Inner Romantic.*

Feed Your Libido includes, as the title implies, those foods providing nutrients essential to maintaining healthy sexual hormone levels. The recipes are packed with ingredients that promote the desire for passion. This chapter probably represents my favorite aspect of my chosen culinary niche. By looking at the nutritional makeup of many foods historically touted as aphrodisiacs, it becomes pretty clear why these ingredients were held in such high regard by cultures around the world in the first place. I love this stuff!

In fact, what I view as one of the most important aspects of my job as an authority on aphrodisiac foods is combining research of folkloric history with modern nutritional science to help promote a diet rich in the essential ingredients for a healthy sex life. Its really all about the old adage, you are what you eat. If you don't give your body the right balance of nutrients for overall health, you can't expect to have a fulfilling romantic life.

For example, without ample zinc you may have problems with blood flow. Without proper blood flow, simply put, orgasm is impossible. This could help explain the aphrodisiac allure of oysters, an easily digestible source of zinc. Vitamin E is also known as the "sex vitamin" because it is believed to aid in the production of sexual hormones. This may be the key to explaining the aphrodisiac history of ingredients like almonds, eggs and mangos. For readers looking to start a libido-boosting diet, in addition to the *Feed Your Libido* recipe chapter, I've provided an entire *Dictionary of Desire*, Chapter 9, to help define the essential nutrients and key ingredients for sexual health for life.

And although the subject of *Feed Your Libido* may be my favorite aphrodisiac food topic, *Unleashing Your Inner Romantic* may be the book's most important recipe chapter. After all, if attraction's going to happen, it will, eventually, happen naturally. But keeping romance alive, as I've learned in the years since meeting Mr. Takeout, that takes work! (It's the most rewarding kind of work, but its work none-the-less.) I also think that letting your inner romantic create the meal and the mood helps to set the scene for those elusive "peak love experiences," those heart-melting, sometimes mind-bending moments we treasure for the rest of our lives.

The recipes in my romance chapter are peppered with ingredients that can potentially cause arousal combined with nutrients important for sexual health. But they're also full of indulgent ingredients perfect for

What is an Aphrodisiac Food?

sharing with someone special. Many of these recipes take a little more time to prepare than those in the book's other chapters. They are designed with the idea in mind that two could share the job, falling into the rhythm of teamwork (which may later translate to the rhythm of the horizontal cha cha). The chapter's filled with the sort of foods that make you feel special when served to you by a significant other. They are intended to indulge taste, sight, smell and touch with rich flavors and colors, intoxicating aromas and sensual textures.

What's most interesting to me about *Unleashing Your Inner Romantic* is how it leads us into the realm of sociology. Even Dr. Liebowitz, a professor of Clinical Psychiatry, maintains that we are wired to form attachments with other humans. And what better way is there to bond and reconnect with others than through cooking? The greatest food writers of our time, including such illustrious wordsmiths as M.F.K. Fisher and Ruth Reichl, offer food memoirs laced with romance and attraction. They don't speak directly of aphrodisiacs but talk of the community of the table, of creating and sharing memories triggered by the smells and tastes of food. Those who translate the delights of the table into the written word understand consciously what we all know on some level: that eating is one of the shared pleasures to which we all can relate. I just tend to take the attitude that, while we're relating, why not have romantic relations?!

While it isn't one of the accepted phases of romance, I believe there's one more stage in which foods can have a profound impact on our romantic lives. And that's in looking for love. Face it, if you don't feel sexy, you can't be sexy. As Dr. Ruth famously quipped, "The most important sex organ lies between the ears."

Historically, foods have been used to make us look and feel more attractive for at least as long as mankind has been keeping records. So I don't think we can discount the use of food to make us look and feel our best as a powerful use of aphrodisiacs. It's a concept I kept in mind while creating nearly every recipe in this book. That's why my meals tend to be lower in fat and calories and offers a greater effort to sneak in extra nutrients whenever possible than the recipes of your average cookbook. But because I think its just as important as the other phases of romance, I've dedicated an entire chapter, Chapter 5, *Super Sexy Me*, to foods that get you primed to enter the games of love.

So many foods are touted for their abilities to make us look younger, feel stronger, glow. So it was easy to put these kinds of ingredients together to create a sexy arsenal. Take, for example, antioxidants, which are constantly incorporated into skin care news stories (although there is now some recent dispute as to how helpful they are in slowing the aging process). But we do know that they go a long way in promoting our overall health. The greatest way to get enough is to incorporate antioxidant-rich foods into your diet. It seems to me a no-brainer that if nibbling more fresh berries, almonds and eggs is going to help you look and feel your most gorgeous, then get cooking and land yourself the man or woman of your dreams.

What is an Aphrodisiac Food?

Now, legend has it that certain other aspects of foods earn them aphrodisiac status. But I'm not really buying that a mere glance at a cucumber, asparagus or geoduck clam will get you in the mood—it certainly wouldn't work for me. And I just can't believe that eating a bull's penis (and other ridiculous animal parts) will transform a man into a bull in heat. That's one I most definitely hope is not true.

As for the FDA, to a degree, I understand why the organization has chosen its stance. This narrow minded definition of aphrodisiacs is designed to protect the consumer from wasting money on "snake oil" or ingesting something as dangerous as Spanish Fly. But I fear that by promoting a message that no food can impact sexual hormones, the FDA diminishes the importance of good diet in attaining and maintaining sexual, not to mention overall, health. (Oh and by the way, a study in 2005 discovered that an amino acid in mussels has the potential for directly raising sexual hormones. So take that, FDA!)

I'm extremely passionate about foods of passion and the fact that the right balance of ingredients can be the key to enjoying one of the most important aspects of human nature and human interaction. If you take nothing else away from this book, I hope you take this: Romancing your stove can bring more sensual, memorable, naughty, fun, fantastic romance into your life, for life.

~2~
Recipes for Seduction

Certain ingredients are perfect to use in planning a meal of seduction because of an immediate, physiological effect. For example, chiles and ginger raise body temperature and promote adrenalin, coffee elevates mood and offers instant energy, etc. This chapter features those kinds of foods, incorporated into recipes suitable for that night you intend to seal the deal, the weekend the kids go to grandma's, or when you find your romance falling into one of those phases when your flame needs reigniting.

love me tender spicy peanut omelet

vegetarian

makes 2 servings

Elvis brought us the pb/banana combo and he certainly smoldered, so surely the pairing can help the rest of us. A peanut butter omelet may sound crazy but I know it works because I stole the idea from one of my all-time favorite breakfast places, The Red Cottage on Cape Cod. The egg, with its neutral flavor acts almost like bread but offers protein for energy. The chili in the peanut butter sauce really heats things up, and the bananas? Ever wonder where the phrase "going bananas" originated?

1. In a small mixing bowl, whisk eggs and egg whites until mixture is thoroughly combined and slightly foamy. Stir in salt.

2. Either divide the beaten eggs into 2 servings to cook 1 at a time or make 1 omelet to share (I vote for the share technique!).

3. In a small pan, melt the butter and swirl pan to coat the entire bottom. (If you are going to make 2 omelets, divide the butter between 2 pans.)

4. Cook the eggs as you would any omelet, drizzling the peanut butter sauce over both servings when the eggs begin to set.

2 eggs*

3 egg whites*

pinch salt

2 tsp butter

1 banana, sliced into rounds

1/2 tsp fresh parsley, finely chopped

2–3 tbsp peanut butter sauce, (recipe below)

5. When the omelet is almost cooked, top half the pan with the sliced banana and parsley then fold the other half over top.

6. Slide the omelet to your serving pan and enjoy. Make it a full meal by adding a couple pieces of smoky turkey bacon and slices of your favorite fresh fruit.

3 tbsp smooth peanut butter, room temperature, (or soften in microwave if it has been refrigerated)

3/4 tsp soy sauce

1 tsp rice wine vinegar

1/4 tsp sriracha

2–3 tbsp hot water

for the peanut sauce:

1. Whisk the peanut butter, soy sauce, rice wine vinegar and sriracha together in a mixing bowl.

2. Slowly add hot water to thin mixture. You may not need to use all of the water.

Leftover peanut sauce makes a tongue tingling, libido lifting dip for chicken, tofu skewers or fresh spring rolls.

grilled oysters with tomatillo salsa
by Amelia Ceja of Ceja Vineyards and Bistro Sabor
serves 4–5 as an appetizer

Some flavors seem made for each other and I believe tomatillo salsa with lime makes one of those perfect culinary marriages. Here, the pairing is served over sensual oysters, perhaps the best-known aphrodisiac of all seafoods. Grilling the oysters lightly adds a smokiness for further depth of flavor. I recommend serving this appetizer with a Sauvignon Blanc, preferably Ceja Sonoma Coast Sauvignon Blanc!—Amelia Ceja

1. Peel the tomatillos' husks and rinse in water. Grill or roast the tomatillos and the jalepenos until the skins appear burned. Do not peel the skins.

*
Tomatillos are found in the produce department of most grocery stores.

1 pound fresh
  tomatillos*

4 fresh jalapeno
  peppers

2 garlic cloves

1/4 c chopped cilantro

salt to taste

4 tbsp unsalted butter

1 tbsp garlic, finely
  minced

20 oysters

1 lime, quartered

Tapatio hot sauce

1–2 tsp Parmesan
  cheese, finely grated

2. In a blender or food processor, combine 2 cloves of garlic, tomatillos and peppers, process until semi-smooth. Add cilantro and salt and process for an additional 8 seconds. Set aside.

3. Combine butter and minced garlic. Melt mixture on the stove or in a microwave. Set aside.

4. Heat grill or broiler to medium. Place the oysters on the hot grill or under the broiler and cook for about 2–3 minutes. Carefully shuck so as not to lose the oysters' juice. (If you like your oysters cooked through, continue to grill until the shells open slightly—this makes them extremely easy to shuck.)

5. To serve, top each with 1/4 tsp garlic butter, 1/2 tsp tomatillo salsa, a squeeze of lime, two drops of Tapatio hot sauce and a pinch of grated Parmesan cheese. Enjoy immediately.

Recipes for Seduction

white truffle scented wild mushroom risotto
recipe by Chef Jack Czarnecki of Joel Palmer House
vegetarian
serves 10 as a small starter or 4 as a main course

Chef Jack Czarnecki is known as a leading American authority on mushrooms—one of my favorite aphrodisiacs. He also happens to be an old family friend. To top it off, Jack is the creator of what is considered one of the finest white truffle oils in the world (one of the few made from real truffles). And since the scent of truffle is known to replicate that of a male pheromone, his contribution makes an undeniably tempting addition to this chapter.

1. In uncovered pan, bring water, mushrooms, sugar, salt and soy sauce to a boil. Strain out the softened mushrooms and reserve liquid. Finely chop the mushrooms.

2. In a medium sauté pan, melt the butter and add the dried onion and rice. Stir for 1 minute.

3. Add the chopped mushrooms and reserved mushroom liquid. Cook uncovered at medium-low heat until water is absorbed and evaporated, stirring occasionally, 15–20 minutes.

4. Portion rice, drizzle lightly with Parmesan cheese and truffle oil (preferably Oregon White Truffle Oil) and serve with a glass of earthy, Oregon Pinot Noir.

1/2 oz dried porcini mushrooms
1 tsp sugar
1 tsp salt
1 tbsp soy sauce
1/3 c unsalted butter
1/2 oz dried onion
1 c arborio or long grain rice
1 oz grated Parmesan cheese
2 oz white truffle oil, (Joel Palmer House Oregon White Truffle Oil preferred)

lemongrass infused
tangerine mimosas,
pg 85

below: huevos style
wake & bake, pg 76

pick-me-up breakfast
parfait, pg 91

below: sultry strawberries
'n' cream buttermilk
pancakes, pg 57

coffee kissed buffalo burgers

makes 4 burgers

Buffalo makes a great alternative to beef. It's lower than beef in cholesterol and calories, higher in protein and iron. You may not consciously realize it but these are things your libido desires. Most buffalo is raised grazing on grass instead of manufactured feed and synthetic hormones. Because it's grown trendy in recent years, buffalo is now widely available and is even sold in many mainstream grocery stores.

1/2 tsp salt

1/2 tsp pepper

2 tsp fine coffee grounds

1 lb ground buffalo, (or 4 buffalo patties)

1/2 sweet onion, cut into rounds

2 tbsp oyster sauce

4 slices ripe tomato, (optional)

2 whole grain sandwich rolls

1. Mix salt, pepper and coffee grounds into the ground buffalo and form 4 burger patties with 1/4-inch thickness.

2. Brush grill with cooking oil and heat to high.

3. Cook burgers for 3–5 minutes per side depending on desired doneness, flipping once. (Because of its low fat content, buffalo will become tough if overcooked.)

4. After burgers are flipped, add onion rounds to the grill. Grill onions 2–3 minutes per side.

5. Top each half of the buns with 1–2 tsp oyster sauce. Add a tomato slice (optional) and 1/4 of the grilled onions. Top with a burger and serve openfaced.

If you are only serving 2 burgers, save the second bun and toppings separately, in the refrigerator, for up to 48 hours.

Recipes for Seduction

The ground buffalo mixture can also be used to make meatballs. Just brown lightly in a sauté pan and serve with pasta or as an appetizer with oyster sauce for dipping.

burgers & wine:

It is well known that a big, bold red wine can take a burger to new aphrodisiac heights. But because I love the unexpected, I recommend trying your burger with a glass of something light and fresh like a Riesling. I think the effect of a bright, white wine dancing across the tongue and washing down the heavier meat has the ability to awaken the senses in a deliciously surprising manner.

hot sausage stew

makes 4 servings

There's nothing like a hot sausage to get the libido going, is there? But the real reason for this dish's amorous effect is found in its aphrodisiac flavorings, including fennel (which is a source not only of plant estrogens but the libido-boosting nutrients of magnesium, iron, vitamin C and manganese).

olive oil for brushing grill

4 Italian-style chicken or turkey sausages

1 red onion, thinly sliced into rounds

1 red bell pepper, cored and thinly sliced

1 yellow bell pepper, cored and thinly sliced

1. Brush grill with olive oil and heat to medium. Grill sausages, turning occasionally until all sides are done, about 12 minutes in total. (Cooking times may vary depending on the sausages.) Remove from heat and set aside.

1 small fennel bulb, trimmed and thinly sliced, (like the onion)

1 tsp paprika

1/2 tsp ground coriander

1/4 tsp salt

1/4 tsp black pepper

2 cloves garlic, finely minced

1 1/2 c dry red wine*

2 tbsp Dijon mustard

1 tsp honey

4 tsp grated pecorino cheese

4 tsp fresh basil, finely chopped

crusty, whole grain bread for mopping up sauce

*

Rather than using cooking wine, which is pretty terrible stuff, why not use a nice, mid-priced bottle of wine in the stew and serve the rest of the bottle to accompany your aphrodisiac feast?

2. Spray a large, nonstick pan with cooking spray and heat to medium-high. Sauté onion until soft, about 3 minutes.

3. Add the peppers and fennel to the pan and sauté, stirring occasionally, until peppers begin to soften, about 10 minutes.

4. Whisk together the paprika, coriander, salt, pepper, garlic, wine, mustard and honey. Add liquid mixture to the pan and simmer, covered, for 10 minutes.

5. Add grilled sausages to the stew and simmer, uncovered for an additional 5 minutes.

6. Season to taste with salt and pepper—but bear in mind that the cheese will give the dish additional saltiness.

7. To serve, arrange a sausage and 1/4 of the pepper mixture to each plate, making sure to scoop up the liquid. Sprinkle each serving with 1 tsp of the cheese and basil and serve with the crusty, whole grain bread.

cupid's kiss champagne cocktail
makes 2 servings

I originally created this drink for a Valentine's Day promotion at a sexy, boutique hotel. We wanted something in a romantic blush color, low enough in alcohol so guests could enjoy a few drinks and still be able to experience the pleasures of their silky sheets. In addition, the cocktail manages to incorporate a few libido-enhancing ingredients into this effervescent little package.

1. Add 1 tbsp fruit syrup to a Champagne flute, top with the Champagne or sparkling wine.

2. Drain and repeat.

for the balsamic fruit syrup:

1. Marinate fruit and 3 tbsp sugar in the balsamic for 30 minutes–1 hour.

2. Taste mixture, and if it is not sweet enough, stir in additional sugar 1 tsp at a time, up to 3 tsp, allowing fruit to marinate for an additional 10 minutes.

3. Strain to remove seeds, pressing fruit against the strainer to release all the juice. Store juice in the refrigerator until serving. (The macerated fruit remaining in the strainer can be saved in a separate container to serve over ice cream or Greek yogurt.)

2 tbsp balsamic fruit syrup

10 oz Brut Champagne or sparkling wine

1/2 c thawed frozen raspberries

1/2 c thawed frozen strawberries

3–4 tbsp granulated sugar

2 tbsp balsamic vinegar

coconut remydy

makes 1 cocktail

My idea with this drink was to find a way to use coconut water's health benefits in a sexy cocktail. Loaded with energizing vitamins and minerals, coconut water is the most hydrating drink on earth. With this recipe, I figured you could boost energy and prevent a hangover while enjoying a cognac glow.

1 1/2 oz Rémy Martin V.S.O.P.

1/3 c coconut water

1 1/4 tsp simple syrup

1 tsp freshly squeezed calamansi juice*

1 wedge calamansi or tangerine

1 sprig fresh mint

1. Combine the Rémy, coconut water, simple syrup and calamansi. Serve, stirred, on the rocks.

2. Garnish with the wedge of fruit and sprig of mint.

for the simple syrup:

1. To make a simple syrup, bring 1/2 cup water to a simmer, add 1/2 cup granulated sugar. Stir until sugar dissolves and chill before using. Store leftover syrup in the refrigerator.

If you can't find calamansi (a tart, Asian citrus), substitute 1 tsp tangerine juice and 1/4 tsp lemon juice.

Recipes for Seduction

seal the deal chipotle-bacon-chocolate chippers

recipe by Tina Casaceli of Milk & Cookies Bakery

makes 24 servings

I love a good cookie—and Tina makes some of the best cookies I've ever tasted. She created this recipe to celebrate chocolate, one of America's favorite aphrodisiacs. She's made them even sexier with the tongue-tingling, smoky taste of chipotle. Although there's little scientific evidence to substantiate it, bacon's amorous effects have been documented throughout history. In Victorian times, it was known to light a woman's inner fire. And today, its scent alone is said to drive men wild. But don't take my word for it; try these cookies for yourself. I think you'll be blown away by Tina's chewy, crunchy, spicy, salty combination. Eaten warm from the oven, while their fragrance still hangs in the air, they are potent little love snacks.

1. Preheat oven to 350 degrees.

2. Lay bacon on a foil or parchment-lined baking sheet and place in oven at 350 degrees for 15 minutes or until bacon is fully cooked and crisp. Remove from pan cool before chopping into bacon bit-sized chunks. Set aside.

3. Measure out 1 2/3 cup oats then process in food processor until finely ground.

*

If cherry wood smoked bacon is unavailable, substitute with another hardwood smoked bacon.

1 c cherry wood smoked bacon*

1 2/3 c old fashioned oatmeal

1 1/3 c all-purpose flour

2/3 tsp baking powder

2/3 tsp baking soda

1/4 tsp salt

1 tsp chipotle powder

1 c unsalted butter

2/3 c granulated sugar

2/3 c brown sugar, firmly packed

1 large egg

1 egg white

1 tsp vanilla extract

12 oz extra bitter (or dark) chocolate chunks (1 bag)

4. Combine ground oats, flour, baking powder, baking soda, salt and chipotle powder. Set aside.

5. Using an electric mixer, beat butter on medium until creamy (2–3 minutes).

6. Gradually add granulated and brown sugars, beat well.

7. Add egg, egg white and vanilla, beating until well blended.

8. Gradually add dry ingredients to butter mixture.

9. Fold in chocolate and bacon.

10. Transfer dough to refrigerator and chill for at least 2 hours.

11. Scoop desired size onto baking sheet and bake for approximately 10 minutes at 350 degrees.

pistachio affogato

vegetarian

makes 2 servings

Affogato is an Italian zinger of a dessert. Traditionally it is made with vanilla gelato. But why go Plain Jane when you can serve up a surprising flavor sensation? The combination of steaming hot coffee with ice cream is goose bump-inducing. A wake up call in a glass, the shot of espresso at the end of the meal will have you skipping off to the bedroom, if you even make it that far!

1. Drop 1/3 cup gelato into each of the two servings of espresso. Serve immediately and make magic.

2/3 c pistachio gelato
2 double espresso*

You can, of course, also try a traditional vanilla bean or chocolate affogato using the proportions above. To take the dish to new aphrodisiac heights, top each serving with a pinch of ground cinnamon.

*

If you don't have an espresso machine, you have two options. Either make the strongest possible coffee using your regular method or pick up espresso from your local haunt and race it home while it's still hot. Either way, you'll have something very sexy to serve to your sweetie.

~3~
Feed Your Libido

One of the most powerful ways you can impact your romantic life with food is by eating the right balance of nutrients for your libido. You may not get an immediate effect from these recipes as you would with the Recipes for Seduction. But when they kick in, you can enjoy some pretty remarkable results (for life) if you keep it up.

I've highlighted a bit about each recipe's most aphrodisiac attributes. However, you can find much more detailed information about the ingredients and the nutrients that will keep your flames of passion burning in my *Dictionary of Desire*.

casanova fruit smoothie

vegetarian

makes 2 servings

There are few ways to get a good dose of fruits and veggies before you even rub the sleep from your eyes. Because everything goes right into the blender, you can make this smoothie in about two minutes flat, get a little nutrition boost and bounce back into bed for a pre-shower play date.

Since you use the pear with the skin on, you're getting a nice dose of fiber, which will help prevent the blood sugar spike and crash a glass of juice can cause. Coupled with manganese-rich spinach and the scent of vanilla, this is the kind of drink with the power to turn any man into a Latin lothario.

1. Add grape juice, spinach, pear, 2 tbsp lemon juice, ginger and vanilla to blender. Purée until smooth.

2. Taste. If smoothie isn't sweet enough, add the agave nectar (it all depends on the sweetness of your pear). For additional tartness, add the last tbsp lemon juice.

3. Add ice cubes and blend on high until smooth and frothy.

4. Divide smoothie between two juice glasses to serve.

1/2 c white grape juice

1/2 c spinach

1 small, ripe bartlett or d'anjou pear (skin on), quartered and cored

2–3 tbsp lemon juice

1 tsp fresh ginger root, minced

1/4 tsp vanilla extract

1 tbsp agave nectar, (optional)

10 ice cubes

thai inspired watermelon salad

recipe by Chef Annette Tomei
of the International Culinary Center
makes 4 servings

Watermelon is sometimes called "nature's Viagra" because one of its nutrients, citrulline, has the power to relax blood vessels in a similar way to a certain prescription medication. Chef Annette, one of my favorite hot chicks in the kitchen, gives watermelon a little exotic flare with this spicy and refreshing salad.

3 tbsp freshly squeezed lime juice

3 c neutral oil, (such as grape seed or canola)

1 tbsp fish sauce

1 1/2 tsp agave nectar or honey

1/2 Thai chile, very thinly sliced, (optional)

salt to taste

4 c watermelon cut into 1-inch cubes

1 c shredded carrot

2–3 scallions, julienned

1/2 c Thai basil leaves, cut into thin ribbons

1 c bean sprouts

1/2 c roasted peanuts, chopped

12 grilled shrimp, (optional)*

1. Whisk together lime juice, oil, fish sauce, agave nectar or honey and (optional) Thai chile, seasoning to taste with the salt. For milder flavor, replace the Thai chile with jalapeno or omit it all together. Alternatively, steep the chile in the dressing for an hour, straining it out before dressing the salad.

2. Arrange watermelon on a serving plate and drizzle with a small amount of dressing. Combine the shredded carrots, scallions, Thai basil and bean sprouts. Dress to taste with remaining dressing, (you may not need it all). Arrange the dressed vegetables over the watermelon, top with chopped peanuts.

3. *Optional:* To create an entrée salad, serve over a bed of lettuce leaves and top each serving with 3 grilled shrimp that have been tossed with the dressing before serving.

Feed Your Libido

garlic soupe d'amour
vegetarian
makes 2–4 servings as an appetizer

Garlic soup is an old, French cure-all. I know, it sounds crazy to center an aphrodisiac dish on garlic. But by roasting the garlic, the flavor becomes sweet, losing much of the pungence that can seep from your pores. Yet it still delivers garlic's health benefits, which, you might be surprised to learn, are many. The ancient Greeks noted that garlic promotes energy and began feeding it to athletes prior to competition. It also offers age-defying antioxidants and may, according to recent research, even be helpful in promoting weight control.

1. Preheat oven to 400 degrees.

2. Remove any loose skin from garlic and roast, whole, in the oven for 20 minutes or until it gives slightly to the touch. Set aside until garlic is cool enough to touch.

1 head garlic, whole
4 c chicken stock
1 tsp fresh or 1/2 tsp dried thyme
salt to taste
4 fresh baguette slices
butter, (optional)

3. In a medium stockpot, bring chicken stock to a simmer.

4. When it is simmering, add in thyme. Squeeze individual garlic cloves from their skins and add to the stock.

5. Simmer for 20 minutes.

6. Pour soup into blender (or use an immersion blender) and purée until soup is smooth.

7. Return to pot and heat through before serving, seasoning with salt to taste. Serve with the baguette slices and (optional) butter.

Feed Your Libido

sizzling mussels in exotic broth

makes 2 servings

For something that looks so impressive on the plate, mussels are incredibly simple to cook. They also happen to be among the seafood world's superfoods when it comes to sex drive. Not only do they make an excellent source of lean protein, a recent study found that mussels may directly raise sexual hormone levels. Not bad for a food that takes about 10 minutes to make.

1. Rinse the mussels well in cold water, discarding any that won't close when handled. If the mussels have not been debearded, remove the patch of seaweed, or "beard," sticking out from between the two shells by pulling with your fingers. If it's stubborn, cut it with a knife.

2. In a small bowl, whisk together the mirin, chicken broth, sriracha and fish sauce.

3. In a nonstick sauté pan or wok, heat the oil over medium-high heat.

4. Sauté the garlic in the oil until edges brown, about 30 seconds.

1 lb mussels

1/2 c mirin* (sweet rice wine)

1/2 c chicken broth

1 tsp sriracha (hot chili sauce)

2 tbsp fish sauce

2 tbsp vegetable oil

1 clove garlic, finely minced

1 tbsp fresh lemon juice

2 scallions, chopped, (optional)

1/4 c cilantro, (optional)

crusty baguette

5. Add the liquid mixture. Bring to a boil and boil for 1 minute.

8. Add the mussels, reducing heat slightly, cover and cook until all the mussels are open, about 4–5 minutes. (They may open sooner.) Remove from heat. Drizzle with lemon juice and top with (optional) scallions and/or cilantro. Or, if you prefer, just eat them naked—the way I like to do it.

9. Divide mussels between 2 bowls and serve with a crusty baguette to sop up the juice.

> *
> If you don't have mirin, substitute with a fruity Sauvignon Blanc or Pinot Grigio.

seared scallop and apple salad with silky sweet potatoes

makes 2 servings

This recipe does require more steps than most in this book but don't doubt for one minute that your labor won't deliver the sweetest reward. The layers of flavor and aphrodisiac ingredients will have your lover begging for more.

for the potatoes:

1. Preheat oven to 375 degrees.

2. In a shallow baking dish coated with nonstick spray, toss the sweet potatoes, cauliflower and whole shallots with the oil and salt.

3. Bake covered for 15 minutes. Uncover and bake for an additional 15 minutes or until potatoes are fork-tender.

4. Transfer vegetables to a blender or food processor and add 1 tbsp of milk. Purée until mixture is smooth, adding additional milk 1 tbsp at a time until purée reaches desired consistency. Season with salt to taste.

5. Serve immediately or reheat before serving.

Note: The purée actually makes 4 servings. It's a versatile, healthy potato dish, so I love having extra on hand for those nights when I'm too busy to cook.

for the scallops:

1. Over medium heat, melt 1 tsp of the butter in a small nonstick pan.

2. When butter is hot (but not brown), add the apples and sauté until fruit browns slightly and just begins to soften. Remove apples from pan and set aside.

3. Add the rest of the butter and allow it to melt before returning the pan to the heat.

2 medium sweet potatoes (skins on), trimmed and cut into 1-inch pieces

1 1/2 c fresh or frozen cauliflower

2 small shallots, peeled and trimmed

2 tsp neutral oil (such as grape seed or canola)

1 tsp salt

3–5 tbsp skim milk

salt to taste

1 tbsp unsalted butter

1 medium Fuji or other crisp apple

8 large, wild sea scallops or shrimp or 8 oz cleaned squid or langoustines, (I prefer scallops but any of the others will work if cooked carefully)*

pinch salt

1/4 c red wine vinegar

1 tbsp Dijon mustard

2 c baby arugula

*

For variety, replace the scallops with shrimp or 8 oz of langoustines. (Langoustines will cook more quickly than scallops.)

4. Pat scallops dry then sprinkle with the pinch of salt. Add to hot pan and cook until golden brown on both sides, turning once, about 3–4 minutes per side.

5. Remove scallops from pan.

6. Turn heat to low and add the vinegar. Deglaze with the vinegar, being sure to scrape off all the cooked bits at the bottom of the pan and stir it all together. Remove from heat and stir in Dijon mustard to make a vinaigrette.

to assemble:

1. Divide 1/2 of the sweet potato purée between two plates. (Save the other half of the sweet potato purée to serve with grilled chicken, pork chops or your other favorite meat.)

2. Top each plate with 1 cup arugula.

3. Divide apple slices and seared scallops between plates then drizzle with the warm dressing.

A super-sensual recipe like this deserves an equally aphrodisiac glass of wine. Because the dish offers a combination of both hearty and delicate flavors on one plate, it welcomes many styles of wine. I enjoy this romantic recipe with a bottle of Brut-style bubbly, Chardonnay, Riesling, Pinot Noir or even Syrah.

chocolate kissed white bean chili

vegetarian

makes 4–6 servings

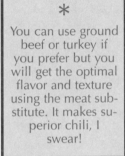

*
You can use ground beef or turkey if you prefer but you will get the optimal flavor and texture using the meat substitute. It makes superior chili, I swear!

There is a long Mexican culinary history of using chocolate in savory dishes. Now, I can't accurately call my recipe Mexican. But what I can call it is aphrodisiac! By layering a tongue-tingling dose of chile pepper with both antioxidant-rich cocoa and bittersweet chocolate, I've given the pot of chili a surprisingly earthy base. To that, I've added a touch of acai, the super-fruit of the Amazon, which brings not only its amazing arsenal of nutrients but offers a subtle sweetness to the final flavor. Because a big bowl of chilli can be a heavy dish, I've omitted meat from the recipe to keep it light. You can use ground meat if you like but I promise you'll love the results from this version.

2 tbsp vegetable oil

1 small yellow onion, chopped

2 stalks celery, chopped

1 clove garlic, finely minced

12 oz soy ground meat substitute*

2 tsp–1 tbsp chile powder

1 tsp ground cumin

1/2 tsp powdered cayenne pepper

1 16 oz can diced tomatoes

1 16 oz can white beans

1 c vegetable broth

1/4 tsp dried oregano

1 bay leaf

1/4 c pure açai juice or fruit purée, (optional)**

1 oz bittersweet chocolate, grated, (or chocolate chips)

1/4 tsp cinnamon

salt to taste

1. Heat vegetable oil in a large stockpot.

2. Sauté onions and celery until soft, about 3 minutes.

3. Add garlic and sauté for an additional minute.

4. Add ground soy, chile powder, cumin and cayenne and sauté for 1 minute.

5. Stir in tomatoes, white beans, vegetable broth, oregano, bay leaf and (optional) açai juice or fruit purée. Bring to a boil then simmer, covered, for 2 hours, stirring occasionally. If chili gets too thick, stir in water 1/2 cup at a time until chili reaches desired thickness.

6. Remove bay leaf and stir in chocolate and cinnamon. Turn off heat and season with salt to taste before serving.

**

Açai juice can be found in the refrigerated section of health food grocers, or sold with the frozen foods as a pure fruit purée. If you can't find the ingredient, you can leave it out, but I think it is the key to this delicious stew.

Feed Your Libido

sexy strawberry-basil "lemonade"
makes 1 cocktail

Limoncello lends this cocktail its signature sweet, tart and zesty lemon taste. To this refreshing, summery flavor, I've added the noted aphrodisiacs of strawberry and basil as well as a touch of vodka just to make the whole thing that much more fun.

1. Finely chop strawberries and basil. (To neatly cut basil, roll the leaf into a tube length-wise. Thinly slice with sharp knife through the width of the roll to make thin ribbons. Then lightly chop the ribbons.)

2. Combine strawberries and basil with sugar in a bowl and refrigerate for 10–15 minutes.

3. Take berry mixture from refrigerator and muddle into a delicious, strawberry pulp. Put the pulp in a rocks glass with 3–4 cubes of fresh ice. Add limoncello, vodka and soda and gently stir. If it's too sweet for your taste, splash with additional soda.

2 ripe strawberries
1 fresh basil leaf
1/4 tsp sugar
3–4 cubes fresh ice*
1.5 oz limoncello
.5 oz vodka
1.5–3 oz club soda

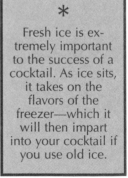

*
Fresh ice is extremely important to the success of a cocktail. As ice sits, it takes on the flavors of the freezer—which it will then impart into your cocktail if you use old ice.

body heat basil-black pepper tea

vegetarian
makes 1 serving

Most of us buy our teas already packaged in neat little pouches. But it can be fun, (not to mention less expensive), to make your own aphrodisiac herbal brew from ingredients in your spice cabinet and your garden. I assembled this unusual flavor combination for its ability to stir up some body heat while tickling the tongue with a complex array of tastes. This flavor trifecta also offers properties to sweeten breath, aid digestion and deliver a dose of antioxidants and vitamin A.

3 black peppercorns, whole

3 cloves, whole

3–4 fresh basil leaves, roughly chopped

1. Crush the black peppercorns slightly so that they break into a few pieces (large enough that they won't slip through a strainer).

2. Put the peppercorns, cloves and chopped basil in a tea ball or strainer and steep in 5–6 oz hot water for 5 minutes or to desired strength.

For a sweet version, stir in a touch of honey or agave nectar before serving.

hand rolled dark chocolate truffles

vegetarian

makes approximately 12 truffles

Studies have shown that a box of chocolates is considered one of the most romantic of all gifts. So imagine presenting your lover with a box of chocolates made by hand...by your hands. You won't even need the libido-boosting attributes of these tiny treats! But for your body's sake, I've filled them with aphrodisiac fruits and rolled them in antioxidant-rich cocoa. I've also cut some of the fat by using half and half instead of cream—you won't even miss it but your arteries might!

*

You can use any dark chocolate bar or bittersweet baking chocolate to make this recipe, but I recommend using a chocolate that has at least 70% cocoa (look for one that tells the percentage on the label).

3 oz premium dark chocolate*

1/3 c half and half

2–3 tbsp your favorite dried fruit (I recommend using blueberries and raspberries)

cocoa powder for dusting

1. Grate chocolate or cut it into chip-sized pieces. (You can also use a premium chocolate chip.)

2. Heat half and half over medium-high heat to a near boil. (Don't let it boil.)

3. Remove pan from heat and whisk in the chocolate, stirring until the mixture is completely smooth.

4. Cool in the refrigerator for about 3–4 hours (or overnight) until chocolate mixture has set.

5. Using a teaspoon, scoop cooled chocolate and form a ball, pressing 1 or 2 pieces of fruit into the center. (Don't waste your time trying to form your truffles into perfect spheres. A slightly uneven surface screams, *"I rolled these chocolates with my own bare hands, expressly for your pleasure."*) If the truffles won't hold shape, refrigerate chocolate mixture for another hour.

6. Cool the formed truffles in the refrigerator for about 5 minutes.

7. Roll each truffle in cocoa powder. Truffles will be soft but if they are so soft that the cocoa is absorbed, store in the refrigerator.

Truffles can be stored in a cool, dry place for up to 5 days.

Feed Your Libido

~4~
Unleashing Your Inner Romantic

As I mentioned in Chapter 1, *What is an Aphrodisiac Food?*, this may be the most important of all the recipe chapters. It's loaded with foods perfect for romantic moments, from breakfast in bed to leisurely summer picnics to indulgent dinners in front of a crackling fire. They are recipes that encourage you to be present in the moment and reconnect. Many are also perfect for cooking together and sharing the experience from beginning to end. Although I've layered the dishes with sensual textures and flavors, that's really only half the recipe. From there, it's up to you to set the stage and take these dishes to new romantic heights.

sultry strawberries 'n' cream buttermilk pancakes

recipe by Chef Bradford Kent of Olio Pizzeria and Café
vegetarian
makes 4 servings

Although he runs a pizzeria, I fell in love with Chef Kent for his brunches, offered only on weekends. Then one morning over breakfast, I learned that he used to run a romantic catering business. A kindred spirit, I asked Brad to contribute one of his lusty breakfast items to the book. Here's what he had to say on his choice, "After a night of passion and morning romance, nothing ignites one's second wind like a shot of coffee and some light, fluffy buttermilk pancakes. These pancakes are best when prepared together and served to one-another by hand, topped with the berries and freshly whipped vanilla cream."

1. Chill the bowl and whisk of an electric mixer.

2. Scrape the pulp from 1/2 the vanilla bean, reserving the rest for another time. Add it to the chilled bowl along with the whipping cream and powdered sugar. Whip until the cream forms soft peaks. Refrigerate until serving.

3. In a medium-size mixing bowl, combine flour, salt, baking powder, baking soda, sugar and cinnamon.

4. Whisk eggs in a large mixing bowl. Add in milk, buttermilk, vanilla and vegetable oil, mixing until thoroughly combined. Fold in the flour mixture and allow batter to rest for 10 minutes.

5. Heat a griddle or heavy skillet over medium heat until it is hot enough to make a few drops of water scatter before evaporating. Brush griddle with vegetable oil and ladle 1/4 cup batter onto the skillet for each pancake.

6. Cook until they bubble on top, about 2 minutes. Flip and cook until golden.

For the sultry experience, feed pancakes to each other straight off the griddle, topping each (or each other) with strawberries, freshly whipped cream and a drizzle of maple syrup.

1 vanilla bean, split lengthwise

1 c whipping cream

2 tbsp powdered sugar, sifted

1 1/2 c all-purpose flour

1/2 tsp salt

2 tsp baking powder

2 tsp baking soda

3 tbsp granulated sugar

pinch cinnamon

2 lg eggs

3/4 c nonfat milk

3/4 c buttermilk

1 tsp vanilla extract

1/4 c vegetable oil

1 c strawberries, thinly sliced

maple syrup

garden tomato & avocado picnic sandwiches

vegetarian

makes 2 sandwiches

I was first introduced to the tomato-avocado sandwich combo in Australia. I liked the flavors so much that I made an art of perfecting this picnic food. I think the sandwich tastes best using a perfectly ripe, Brandywine heirloom tomato, Hass avocado and supercrunchy, seed bread. But it works with any tomato, avocado and whole grain, so long as the tomato is in season and ripe. You're going to be tempted to omit the butter. Don't do it. The thin layer of butter acts as a barrier between tomato and bread, preventing your masterpiece from going all soggy.

4 slices whole grain bread

1–1 1/2 tsp whipped or softened butter

10 slices garden tomato, (about 1 medium tomato)

salt and black pepper to taste

1/2 avocado

1–2 butter lettuce leaves, (optional)

1. Thinly spread 2 slices of bread with the butter. (Use just enough butter to cover the slice.)

2. Top each buttered slice with tomato slices.

3. Sprinkle the tomato with salt and pepper to taste.

4. Remove skin from the avocado and mash to a chunky paste.

5. Spread half the avocacdo on each of the 2 remaining bread slices.

6. Form sandwiches, adding lettuce if you choose. Cut in half and either serve immediately or pack up for a picnic. (Sandwiches will last for about 4 hours.)

Unleashing Your Inner Romantic

grilled scallops with sweet chili sauce

recipe by Chef Brad Farmerie of PUBLIC
and Saxon + Parole
serves 8 as an appetizer or 4 as a main course

As I mentioned in the introduction, Chef Brad Farmerie's style of cooking has been a great influence on this book. So I'm particularly honored to feature a recipe by the man himself. I will warn you, it is one of the book's most challenging recipes and uses the widest array of exotic ingredients, but that's part of its magic. So slap an apron around your lover and play chef together. The results will be so very worth it!

For the chili sauce:

The sauce should be made in advance. The recipe makes more than you will need for one batch of scallops but it will keep in the refrigerator for several months. Because it's a bit time consuming, Brad recommends using leftover sauce to top anything grilled (or to lick off your lover's fingers and toes).

1. Sterilize 2–3 canning jars and lids.

2. In a food processor, combine garlic, ginger, galangal, chiles, lime leaves, lemongrass, beets and cilantro. Process to a smooth purée.

30 cloves garlic, minced

1 c fresh ginger, peeled and minced

3/4 c galangal, peeled and minced

5 red chiles, chopped

10 kaffir lime leaves, finely chopped

4 lemongrass stalks, bruised and finely chopped

heaping 1/3 c roasted beets, peeled and puréed

1/2 c cilantro leaves, chopped

2 1/4 c sugar

1/2 c water

1/4 c and 2 tsp soy sauce

3/4 c cider vinegar

1/3 c fish sauce

1/3 c tamarind water*

*

To make your own tamarind water, combine 2 lg dried tamarind pods with the hard shell removed with 3/4 cup water in a small pot. Bring to a boil. Cover and cook over medium heat for 30 minutes, mashing tamarind occasionally. Strain before using.

16 large scallops, (Brad prefers dry-packed)

neutral oil, such as canola, for brushing

salt and pepper to taste

4 bunches watercress, washed and patted dry

1 c sweet chili sauce

1 c crème fraîche

3. In a heavy pot, combine the sugar and water. Over medium heat, bring to a boil. Continue to cook, stirring until mixture becomes a rich, golden brown, about 8 minutes. (Be careful not to touch the hot sugar.)

4. Working quickly, add the puree to the sugar then stand clear and have the lid ready in case the mixture starts to splatter.

5. After 1–2 minutes, stir with a long, metal spoon. Then reduce to a simmer and cook 5 minutes.

6. Add the soy sauce, cider vinegar, fish sauce and tamarind water and simmer for 15 minutes before transferring to sterile jars.

Store in the refrigerator.

To prepare the scallops:

1. Preheat grill to medium-high.

2. Lightly oil scallops and season with salt and pepper.

3. Place scallops on hot grill and char bottoms, about 2–3 minutes. Do not move them prematurely.

4. When just medium rare, flip and cook other side to medium-well, another 2–3 minutes. (Be sure not to overcook or scallops will become tough.)

5. Divide watercress among serving plates and arrange in center of each plate. Top each with scallops. Place a dollop of chili sauce on each scallop then finish with a dollop of crème fraîche.

pomegranate roasted pork loin with quinoa and sexy veg

makes 4–6 servings

Pomegranate is one of the most notorious aphrodisiac foods in the world. And while this scarlet fruit is the dish's star flavor, it is only one of many potent aphrodisiac ingredients. Sweet potatoes and fennel, both noted libido-lifters, are taken to a whole new level by roasting in sweet pomegranate butter. And quinoa, the good-for-you grain, gets a flavor transformation from breath-sweetening mint. Because this dish requires several steps, it's perfect for cooking together, working side-by-side with the one you love.

1. Place shallot in a Ziplock bag with 1 cup pomegranate juice and 1/4 tsp salt. Remove pork from the refrigerator, add to the bag and marinate on the counter for 30 minutes. (This will allow the pork to come almost to room temperature before cooking.)

2. Preheat oven to 400 degrees while you make the pomegranate butter (recipe below).

3. Cut sweet potato and parsnip into uniform, 1/2-inch pieces. Chop fennel and onion into 1/2-inch long slices. Put the vegetables into a roasting pan and toss with the garlic and 2 tbsp of the pomegranate butter (recipe below).

4. Add the pork to the pan and cook, uncovered, for 30–45 minutes, until a meat thermometer reads 138 degrees.

1 shallot, finely minced

1 c pomegranate juice

1/4 tsp salt

1–1 1/4 lb loin of pork

1 medium, sweet potato

3 parsnips

1 bulb fennel

1 medium, yellow onion

1 clove garlic, finely minced

1 tbsp pomegranate kernels, (optional)

5. Remove the meat from the pan and cover with foil. Allow loin to rest for 15 minutes.

6. Test vegetables with a fork. If they do not feel tender, return pan to the oven while meat is resting.

7. Slice meat thickly and serve over the quinoa (recipe below) with the vegetables as garnish. Drizzle with remaining pomegranate butter to taste. (You may choose not to use all the butter. Any leftovers can be served over grilled chicken or steaks.) Sprinkle with pomegranate kernels (optional).

1 c pomegranate juice

1/4 c white wine

1 shallot, finely minced

4 tbsp unsalted butter, cold

salt to taste

For the pomegranate butter:

1. In a small saucepan, bring the juice, wine and shallot to a boil and reduce to approx 2 tbsps. Turn heat to low and whisk in butter 1 tbsp at a time. Season with salt to taste.

1 c quinoa

1 tbsp lemon juice

1 tbsp olive oil

salt to taste

1/4 c fresh mint, chopped

For the quinoa:

1. Add quinoa to a saucepan with 2 cups water and bring to a boil. Turn heat to low, cover and cook for 10–15 minutes until quinoa has softened and is fluffy but still has texture. (Overcooking quinoa will produce something the texture of grits.)

2. When quinoa is cooked, remove from heat and cool for 20 minutes. Toss with lemon juice and oil and season with salt to taste. Toss in the mint just before serving.

Unleashing Your Inner Romantic

lobster pasta in champagne-tarragon sauce

makes 2 servings

If there could possibly be anything to improve upon the sweet, succulent taste of lobster, it would have to be Champagne and tarragon butter. This is one of my most decadent recipes, so don't just do it halfway. Invest in the highest-quality ingredients, cook with love and serve aside chilled flutes of something bubbly. (You might also want to clear your calendar. If your lover likes lobster, you're going to be busy for a while.)

4 oz dried buckwheat (soba) or whole wheat noodles

2 tsp unsalted butter

1 shallot, minced

2/3 c sparkling wine

1 tbsp fresh tarragon or 3/4 tsp dried

1 tbsp fresh lemon juice

5–6 oz lobster, (approximately 1 large tail), cut into bite-sized pieces

1 c fresh arugula

salt to taste

2 tbsp crème fraîche

2 tsp flying fish caviar (tobiko)*

1. Bring a pot of water to a boil. Cook pasta according to package instructions.

2. Melt butter in a nonstick sauté pan over medium heat. Sauté shallot until soft, about 1–2 minutes. Add sparkling wine, tarragon and lemon juice and bring to a simmer.

3. Turn heat to medium-low and add lobster, simmering until cooked through, about 5 minutes.

4. Remove from heat and immediately add arugula, tossing until it begins to wilt.

5. Season with salt to taste.

To serve:

Divide pasta between 2 plates. Top each with half of the lobster and sauce. Garnish with 1 tbsp crème fraîche with 1 tsp of flying fish roe.

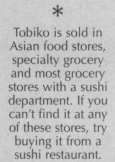

*
Tobiko is sold in Asian food stores, specialty grocery and most grocery stores with a sushi department. If you can't find it at any of these stores, try buying it from a sushi restaurant.

above: sizzling mussels in exotic broth, pg 46; *above right:* shucking oysters for grilled oysters with tomatillo salsa, pg 30; *below:* olive oil poached salmon with sensual spices, pg 65

steamy artichokes skinny dipping in honey, pg 93

above: surprise someone soybean dip, pg 107; *right:* bikini bread, pg 105

garden tomato
& avocado picnic
sandwiches, pg 59

below left: fresh corn soup,
pg 92; *below:* feta & basil
stuffed mushrooms, pg 111

olive oil poached salmon with sensual spices

by Chef James Boyce of Boyce Restaurant Concepts (Cotton Row, Commerce Kitchen and Pane e Vino Pizzeria)

makes 4 servings

I was incredibly honored to have Chef Boyce contribute a recipe to my book. Not only is he one of America's finest chefs, he was one of the first American culinary trendsetters to simplify ingredients and intensify the health benefits of fine dining. Chef Boyce selected this salmon dish not only for its blend of aphrodisiac aromatics but because the spice massage, coupled with the olive oil bath, turns salmon into something positively sensual.

2 lg cloves garlic, pressed or finely chopped and sprinkled with kosher salt

1 tsp garam masala

1 tsp cumin seed, toasted and crushed

1 tsp coriander seed, toasted and crushed

1 tsp salt

1/4 tsp cayenne pepper

2–3 c olive oil

4 4oz, center cut salmon filets, at least 1-inch thickness

2 c cooked white or brown rice

lemon or lime slices to garnish

1. Mix garlic, garam masala, cumin seed, coriander seed, salt and cayenne in a small bowl, adding enough olive oil to make a smooth paste. Massage both sides of each salmon filet with the paste. Allow fish to rest at room temperature for 1 hour.

2. Preheat oven to 225 degrees.

3. Pour olive oil into a baking dish just big enough to fit all 4 salmon filets (pyrex works well), estimating enough oil to cover the fish and heat in the oven for 5 minutes.

4. Submerge salmon in the heated oil and slowly poach in the oven for 25 minutes. Remove fish from oil and serve over rice with lemon and/or fresh lime slices. (Once cooled, the oil can be strained through a coffee filter and refrigerated for up to 3 weeks to reuse as a poaching liquid.)

pomme d'amour champagne cocktail

recipe by Chef Philippe Rispoli of PB Boulangerie Bistro
makes 1 cocktail

Chef Philippe Rispoli has worked for some of the most legendary chefs in the world. But when he opened his own restaurant on Cape Cod, his passion for his homeland of France was in evidence. His is the sort of bistro you imagine in Marseilles where couples meet for illicit affairs, legs entangled as they sip potent drinks and slurp local oysters. I wanted to include one such potent cocktail in hopes that its romantic name and aphrodisiac ingredients will transport you to that place where desire freely flows.

1. Pour vodka, pomegranate liqueur and St. Germain liqueur into a chilled martini glass.

2. Carefully top with Champagne.

3. Garnish with fresh raspberry.

1 oz Chambord raspberry vodka, chilled

1/2 oz pomegranate liqueur

1/2 oz St. Germain elderflower liqueur

Brut Champagne or sparkling wine, well-chilled

fresh raspberry for garnish

hot chocolate martini

makes 2 servings

I wanted to see what would happen if I took the sophistication of a martini, the comfort of a childhood favorite like hot chocolate and swirled it all together. I think the results not only draw on classic flavor memories but leave a lasting impression that is elegant and most definitely adult.

cocoa powder for the rim

1 c hot soymilk, (or regular milk)

1 tbsp dark chocolate, grated

1 oz vanilla vodka

2 oz chocolate vodka

1. Put a small amount of cocoa powder on a plate or saucer. Wet the rim of two martini glasses with soymilk. Roll the rim in the cocoa to make an even coating around the whole rim.

2. Add dark chocolate to the hot soymilk, stirring until melted. (You can use any candy counter chocolate but I recommend choosing a bar with a high percentage of cocoa, at least 65% or 70%, for a really rich, chocolate flavor.)

3. Stir in vanilla and chocolate vodkas then pour into 2 martini glasses. Serve immediately.

Unleashing Your Inner Romantic

creamy lemon custard cakes with rosemary

vegetarian

makes 4 mini cakes

What's impressive about these tart, individual desserts is that they magically separate into cake and custard layers in the oven—all on their own! Despite being relatively low-calorie, their flavors are complex and the texture is like a little pillow of culinary heaven. You might never have thought of adding rosemary to a dessert but used in a small amount, it adds an interesting herbal—but not savory—dimension.

1. Preheat oven to 350 degrees.

2. Coat 4 individual custard or soufflé cups with non-stick cooking spray.

3. Separate eggs. Make sure the egg whites are at, or close to, room temperature or you'll never achieve the desired fluffy clouds you are about to create.

4. Beat the whites to a foamy state, then slowly add in 1/4 cup sugar while continuing to beat until glossy, soft peaks form. (Do not overbeat.)

5. In a separate bowl, combine remaining sugar with butter and beat until thoroughly mixed.

6. Add flour, citrus juice, zest, rosemary and salt to the butter and sugar mixture. Beat at a medium-high speed until thoroughly blended.

7. Stir in egg yolks and milk to form a batter.

2 large eggs, room temperature

1/4 c and 2 tsp granulated sugar

1 tbsp butter, softened

3 tbsp all-purpose flour

3 tbsp lemon juice

2 tsp tangerine juice

1/2 tsp lemon zest

1/4 tsp tangerine zest

1 tsp rosemary, minced

1/4 tsp salt

3/4 c and 2 tsp 2% milk*

*

You can use skim milk for the recipe but I find that the small amount of fat improves the texture of both the custard and cake portions of the dish.

8. Fold 1/4 of the soft peaked egg whites into the batter. With gentle strokes, continue to gradually fold in the egg whites until all the whites have been combined into the batter. If you handle the egg whites roughly, you will lose the ethereal quality of the final cakes.

9. Divide the batter among the 4 cups.

10. Place the cups in a shallow baking dish with about 1-inch warm water. The water will allow the cakes to steam and rise gently in the oven.

11. Bake the cakes for 35 minutes or until the custards are set and the tops lightly golden.

12. Remove cups from pan. Chill for at least 30 minutes or until cups feel cold and custard is completely set.

13. To serve, invert the cakes onto individual plates. The bottom of each cake will be a light angel food topped by a golden custard dome.

Because they aren't very sweet, I recommend trying these cakes with a dry white wine like a Sauvignon Blanc. It really adds to the unexpected element of the whole dessert experience.

lady killer chocolate layer cake

vegetarian

makes 10–12 servings

This rich, moist, multilayered cake is one of my absolute favorite desserts and one that makes most women swoon. It is actually a variation on a vegan cake recipe created by Chrysta Wilson for her Kiss My Bundt Bakery. But instead of topping the cake with vegan buttercream, I arrange it in 4 layers, sandwiched with light cream cheese frosting. The result is not only visually impressive, the super-moist layers are as rich as fudge and, I think, as satisfying without being overly sweet. Unlike most baked goods, this one gets better with age. Store in the refrigerator and serve 24 hours after frosting for a total cakegasm.

1 3/4 c sugar*

2 c all-purpose flour

3/4 c high-fat cocoa powder**

1 1/4 tsp baking powder

1 1/4 tsp baking soda

3/4 tsp salt

1 c unsweetened soymilk

1/3 c vegetable oil

2 tsp vanilla extract

2 tbsp instant coffee granules

3/4 c water, boiling

1. Preheat oven to 350 degrees.

2. Sift together sugar, flour, cocoa powder, baking powder, baking soda and salt. Set aside.

3. Add soymilk, oil and vanilla to a mixing bowl. Using an electric mixer, beat on medium speed for 1 minute.

4. With the mixer on low speed, add dry ingredients to the wet, 1/2 cup at a time. Do this slowly so that the batter doesn't become lumpy.

5. When thoroughly combined, dissolve instant coffee granules into the boiling water. Slowly mix the boiling coffee into the batter by hand, stirring until completely combined.

*

To make a vegan version of the cake, simply use vegan sugar, found at most health food stores. To make a vegan frosting, use vegan powdered sugar and a nondairy cream cheese substitute.

3 oz unsalted butter, softened

8 oz Neufchatel cream cheese, softened

2 c powdered sugar, sifted

1/2 tsp vanilla extract

6. Transfer batter to 2 round cake pans that have been coated with a baker's cooking spray that includes flour (or greased and floured).

7. Bake cakes until an inserted toothpick or cake tester comes out clean—about 18–23 minutes (time may vary by oven).

8. Invert cakes onto a cooling rack or serving plate. If cakes resists, cool in the pan for 15 minutes before inverting. Cool completely before frosting.

for the frosting:

1. With an electric mixer on medium speed, cream the butter and the cream cheese until soft and completely smooth, about 2–3 minutes.

2. Turn the mixer speed to low and slowly add the powdered sugar 1/2 cup at a time, making sure to scrape down any frosting stuck to the sides of the bowl.

3. When sugar is fully incorporated, add vanilla.

4. Mix on a medium speed until frosting is smooth and fluffy.

to assemble:

1. Slice each of the cakes into 2 rounds (so that you will have 4 layers in total). You can cut the cakes with a bread knife, but to easily cut the cakes into nearly perfect disks, stick a toothpick horizontally into the side of the cake half way from the top of the round. Take a 20-inch piece of unflavored, wax-free dental floss. Wrap the floss around the cake just above your toothpick marker. Cross the floss as if you were tying a bow. Keep pulling the floss until the floss has cut the entire first layer.

2. Repeat with the second round.

3. Spread 1/4 of the frosting evenly across the top of the first round (the one on your serving plate). Do NOT ice down the sides of the cake or you will run out of frosting.

4. Top with a cake round and frost the top of this round, repeating with the third round.

5. Add the top layer of cake and spread a very thin layer of frosting. This is your "crumb coat." (The crumb coat will help prevent specks of dark cake in the white frosting on the finished cake.) Refrigerate cake for 15–30 minutes then frost the top of the cake with the remaining frosting.

~5~
Super Sexy Me

Sometimes the best aphrodisiac is feeling great. Why bother with the seductive meal if you can't bear the idea of throwing off all your clothes? Since I think most diet food is weirdly artificial or altogether boring, I've whipped up a set of recipes to increase your pleasure without enlarging your girth. They aren't diet dishes in the traditional, restrictive sense. But they are healthy, reasonably low calorie, low fat choices packed with ingredients to help you achieve glowing skin, optimal energy and, hopefully, a few hormone-enhancing nutrients to get you and keep you in the mood for love.

wake & bake breakfast eggs

vegetarian

makes 4 servings

I love breakfast foods. But what I don't love is the crawling out of bed to chop, sauté and stir so we can lavish a lover with a tray of breakfast treats. So I created the Wake and Bake, an aphrodisiac breakfast that can be prepped up to 24 hours in advance. You just go from fridge to oven and hop back in bed to keep someone warm until your breakfast has baked.

1. Coat a nonstick pan with cooking spray. Over medium heat, sauté zucchini, bell pepper, shallot, garlic, oregano and 1/4 tsp salt for 3–4 minutes, until zucchini is soft and shallot begins to brown. Remove from heat and stir in lemon zest.

2. In a separate bowl, stir together flour and milk with a whisk until mixture is lump free.

3. Add Egg Beaters and salt to milk mixture, whisking until thoroughly combined. Gently stir in Brie.

4. Coat an 8"x 8" baking dish with cooking spray. Spread vegetable mixture in the bottom of the pan. Pour egg mixture over the top. Cover with plastic wrap and hold in the refrigerator. Dish can be kept, refrigerated, overnight.

2 small zucchini, chopped

1 yellow bell pepper, chopped

1 medium shallot, minced

1 clove garlic, minced

1/4 tsp dried oregano

1/2 tsp salt

1 tsp lemon zest

2 tbsp all-purpose flour

3 tbsp milk

1 1/2 c Egg Beaters or other liquid eggs

2 oz ripe Brie cheese (rind on), cut into 1/4-inch pieces

2 tbsp Gruyère cheese, grated, (added during cooking)

Optional additional ingredients/alterations: add 1 tsp chopped, fresh chives or 1 tsp chopped, fresh basil to the egg mixture; replace 1 zucchini with 1 yellow squash or 1 c chopped, fresh spinach; add ham, smoked salmon or veggie ham to the eggs; use truffle salt instead of table salt.

to bake:

5. Preheat oven to 325 degrees.

6. Bake, uncovered, for 22–25 minutes or until eggs are just set (once you can shake the pan and it doesn't jiggle). (Baking time may take slightly longer in a glass baking dish.)

7. Remove from oven and sprinkle with Gruyère. Put the baking dish under the broiler for an additional 3–4 minutes, until the top has turned golden brown.

8. Cut into squares and serve warm or at room temperature.

If you love your carbs in the morning, stack your eggs on a slice of whole grain toast and garnish the plate with seasonal fruit.

Super Sexy Me

huevos style wake & bake

(a spicy variation on the Wake and Bake)
vegetarian
makes 4 servings

1. Follow instructions for cooking the vegetables but stir in 3 tbsp salsa and the chile powder with the lemon zest.

2. In step 3, use 2 tbsp grated Cheddar or Jack in place of the Brie.

3. In step 6, eggs will cook slightly longer, 24–28 minutes to bake.

4. In step 7, top with Cheddar or Jack in place of Gruyère.

5. To serve, garnish each egg square with 1 tbsp salsa and 1 tsp light sour cream.

additional ingredients:
7 tbsp your favorite salsa, divided

1/2 tsp chile powder

4 tbsp grated sharp Cheddar or Jack cheese, divided

4 tsp light sour cream

ingredient adjustments:
omit Brie

omit Gruyère

If you'd like some carbs with that, try toasting a couple of all natural corn tortillas and serve with additional salsa for dipping.

succulent shrimp in a rosemary salt crust
makes 2 servings

Roasting shrimp in salt is deceptively easy—almost a parlor trick. Its a great choice for date night, since not only will your cooking chops impress without your ever breaking a sweat but you're serving a dish that has to be eaten with your fingers, (always a sexy experience).

What I most love about this recipe is that it introduces you to a totally fat free and figure-friendly yet exceedingly succulent cooking method. Packing seafood in salt (you can also use this technique for roasting whole fish) locks in the moisture but the shell, or in the case of fish the skin, prevents the sodium from leaching into the meat. Best of all, the cooking vessel is all natural and the cleanup couldn't be quicker.

1. Preheat oven to 500 degrees.

2. Spread half the salt on the bottom of a baking dish (8"x 8" or a small casserole will work).

3. Heat the pan of salt in the oven for 5 minutes. (This will help ensure quick, even cooking.)

4. Lay a bed of rosemary on top of the salt.

5. Arrange shrimp in a single layer on top of the rosemary.

6. Cover with remaining salt.

7. Bake for 10 minutes, then let the dish rest for 2 minutes before removing shrimp from salt and serving warm. (Do not let shrimp rest in salt for more than 5 minutes.)

Serve naked or with your favorite dipping sauce. (Olive oil sautéed with a bit of minced garlic is a nice choice.)

3–4 c coarse salt

4–5 sprigs fresh rosemary

12 jumbo shrimp or prawns, unpeeled*

---

*

You can also use whole prawns with the heads intact. The presentation is a knockout.

grilled chicken spinach salad
with plump peaches
makes 2 servings

This recipe is a summertime favorite of Mr. Take-out's. And I love how little time the prep takes for such a sweet, salty, crunchy, silky tease to the senses. The salad is at its best on a hot, summer day when peaches are at their peak of freshness. But you can try it at other times of the year with each season's finest fruit, like apricots in late spring and figs in the fall.

2 4 oz boneless, skinless chicken breasts

1/2 c dry white wine

olive oil for brushing

1 pinch salt

1/2 medium red onion, sliced into rounds

1 large peach, pitted and sliced into 8 wedges

4 c fresh baby spinach

2 tsp flax seed oil

salt and pepper to taste

1. Marinate chicken breasts in dry white wine for 30 minutes–1 hour, turning once.

2. Brush grill with oil and heat to medium-high heat.

3. Sprinkle each chicken breast with salt and grill for 5 minutes.

4. When the chicken has cooked for 5 minutes, turn to cook for an additional 4–5 minutes and add onion slices and peach wedges to the grill.

5. After 2 minutes, flip the onions and peaches.

6. While the chicken is cooking, toss spinach with flax seed oil and divide between two plates. Season with salt and pepper to taste.

7. To serve, top each plate of spinach with a hot chicken breast. Arrange 4 peach wedges and half the onions on each plate. Serve warm.

Super Sexy Me

herb massaged london broil with simple grilled asparagus

makes 4–6 servings

In general, beef is a notoriously anti-aphrodisiac ingredient. If you are about to cry out in protest, consider this: What do you feel like doing after eating a big steak? Taking a big nap! But I realize that a lot of people really love red meat. So for all of you, I'm recommending London Broil. Despite some confusion, London Broil is actually a cooking method, not a cut of beef. It uses less tender, lower fat cuts—usually flank steak but you can also use top round. Because of the meat's toughness, I marinate it in red wine. The acidity in the wine will help give the beef a succulent tenderness. Then, I massage it with a fresh herb rub to give it a hint of aphrodisia.

If you like the rub, try using it on anything you wish from pork loin to turkey thighs, human thighs.... Let your imagination be your guide.

1. Trim meat of all visible fat.

2. Let London Broil marinate, refrigerated in red wine for 1–2 hours.

3. Remove meat form marinade. Pat dry and transfer to a broiler pan. Allow meat to come to room temperature (about 45 minutes).

4. Combine rub ingredients (coarse salt, black pepper, sage, thyme, rosemary and shallot) and thoroughly coat meat.

1 London Broil, 1 1/4 to 1 1/2 lbs, (about 1 1/4-inch thick)

1 c dry red wine

2 tsp coarse salt

1/2 tsp black pepper

1 tbsp fresh sage, chopped

1 tbsp fresh thyme

2 tbsp fresh rosemary, chopped

1 medium shallot, minced

1 lb asparagus, ends trimmed

salt to taste

5. Turn broiler to high and broil meat approximately 8 inches under the flame for 7–8 minutes per side, turning once, for medium rare to medium doneness.

for the asparagus:
1. Coat grill or stovetop grill pan with a little cooking oil then heat to medium-high.

2. Cook asparagus for 3–5 minutes depending on thickness, turning once.

3. Remove from grill and season with salt.

Serve with a glass of earthy red wine like a Bordeaux and some roasted sweet potatoes. Or try it with my silky sweet potatoes, page 47.

black truffle lovers' lasagna
vegetarian
makes 4 servings

The scent of black truffle is very similar to that of a male pheromone. (Pheromones are human, sexual scents that unconsciously register as attraction in possible mates.) And I know women who swear by as little as a single whiff of truffles as producing the...ahem... desired effect. Because most of us can't afford to run out and buy black truffles every time we're looking for action, I've created a dish that uses black truffle oil and salt in such a way that it releases that aroma of desire into the air.

1. Sprinkle the eggplant with the 1/2 tsp salt, set aside for 10 minutes. (Eggplant will discolor slightly.)

2. Preheat oven to 375 degrees, and coat an 8 or 9-inch square baking dish with nonstick cooking spray.

3. Heat black truffle-infused oil in a large, nonstick pan over medium heat. Sauté garlic for 1 minute.

4. Add mushroom and sauté for an additional minute.

5. Stir in eggplant and zucchini. Gently sauté for 10 minutes, until vegetables are softened.

6. Stir in spinach and truffle salt then remove from heat when the spinach begins to wilt.

7. Add basil and ricotta and thoroughly mix.

8. Spread 1/4 of the vegetable mixture on the bottom of the baking dish. Top with 2 noodles, followed by 1/4 of the vegetables; then 2 more noodles, repeat, then finish with the last 1/4 of the vegetables.

9. Top with grated Parmesan, cover pan with foil and bake for 20 minutes.

10. Uncover and cook for an additional 5 minutes. For a crunchy top, put under the broiler for an additional 3–5 minutes, until cheese is deep golden.

1 1/2 c eggplant, chopped

1/2 tsp salt

2 1/2 tsp black truffle-infused oil

1 clove garlic, crushed

1 portabella mushroom cap, minced

2 medium zucchini, chopped

2 c baby spinach salad leaves, roughly chopped

1 tsp black truffle salt

1 tbsp fresh basil, chopped

1 c part skim ricotta

6 no-cook lasagna noodles

1/4 c Parmesan, grated

seared halibut with wild mushroom cream in bed with braised celery

makes 4 servings

Most people can't believe that soymilk can be used successfully as a substitute for cream. But soymilk has a sweetness and silky quality not dissimilar to cream. And since this recipe uses so little, you can serve it at a dinner party and I doubt any of your guests will ever notice that what they're tasting is soy. Like soy, celery has plant estrogens, making this dish a great choice for the ladies.

> ✳
> I like a combination of chanterelles and/or morels with oyster mushrooms and crimini.

1 lb assorted mushrooms*

1 tsp unsalted butter

1 shallot, finely chopped

1 pinch salt

1/3 c soymilk

4 halibut steaks, 4 oz each

salt and pepper

1 batch braised celery, (next page)

1 tbsp parsley, finely chopped

1. Clean, trim and slice mushrooms.

2. Heat butter in a sauté pan over medium heat.

3. Sauté shallots for 1 minute.

4. Add mushrooms and a pinch of salt to the pan and sauté for 3 minutes.

5. Turn the heat to low, add the soymilk and simmer for 4 minutes, stirring occasionally.

6. Sprinkle both sides of the halibut with salt and pepper.

7. Sear the halibut over medium heat in a nonstick pan coated with cooking spray. Cook for 3–4 minutes per side, turning once.

8. To serve, put 4 celery pieces on each plate. Top with a halibut steak and 1/4 of the mushroom mixture, making sure to spoon a little cream over each steak. Garnish with parsley.

Super Sexy Me

You can also serve mushroom "cream" over baked chicken breasts, seared salmon and roasted loin of pork.

for the braised celery:
1. Trim celery and cut each stalk in half on a diagonal.
2. Melt butter in a sauté pan over medium heat. Sauté celery for 3 minutes.
3. Add in stock and simmer, covered, for 5 minutes.
4. Uncover and cook for an additional 3 minutes.

Braised celery is also a great accompaniment to simple, grilled seafoods and wild game.

lemongrass infused tangerine mimosas

makes 2 mimosas

In Asian cultures, lemongrass has been linked with libido. (And I also like the eye-opening, herbal element it added to this traditional drink.) Mimosas in general are a great choice of cocktail as they're lower in alcohol and calories than most mixed drinks and they offer that extra hit of vitamin C.

2 tsp lemongrass syrup

4 oz tangerine or orange-tangerine juice

7–8 oz Brut Champagne or sparkling wine

2 stalks lemongrass, cut into 2-inch sections

1/4 c granulated sugar

1/2 c water

1. In each of two Champagne flutes, add 1 tsp lemongrass syrup and 2 oz tangerine or orange-tangerine juice.

2. Top each flute with 3 1/2 or 4 oz chilled Champagne or sparkling wine.

for the lemongrass syrup:

1. Add all 3 ingredients to a small saucepan. Bring to a boil then simmer for 30 minutes (depending on the size of your saucepan) or until liquid reduces by 1/2. (If your saucepan is large, keep an eye on the simmering mixture to ensure it doesn't scorch the pan.)

2. Remove from heat and allow syrup to steep until cool.

3. Strain out lemongrass and chill before using.

Leftover syrup can be used as a tangy substitute for simple syrup in any recipe.

Super Sexy Me

chocolate-almond seduction cookies

vegetarian

makes approximately 24 cookies

I've been working for years to develop a cookie recipe that's light on fat and calories but still has great texture. The trick, I've discovered, is to keep some of the fat, which is essential for "mouth feel." The final recipe uses applesauce to replace some (but not all) of the butter and then uses egg white for volume and body. It only recently occurred to me to add almond meal to give the cookies a little aphrodisiac nutrition—including a dose of vitamin E (the sex vitamin!).

1. Combine flour, almond meal, baking soda, salt and cocoa in a small mixing bowl. Set aside.

2. In a mixing bowl, stir butter until creamy. Add the sugars and mix until combined, about 1 minute by hand. Then add applesauce, vanilla, almond extract and egg white, stirring for an additional 2 minutes.

3. Add the flour mixture, stirring until thoroughly combined.

4. Fold in the chocolate chips.

2/3 c all-purpose flour

1/3 c almond meal

1/4 tsp baking soda

1/4 tsp salt

1/2 c high-fat cocoa powder, sifted

4 tbsp unsalted butter, softened

1/2 c brown sugar, packed

1/2 c granulated sugar

3 tbsp unsweetened applesauce

1/2 tsp vanilla extract

1/2 tsp almond extract

1 large egg white

3/4 c dark chocolate chips

5. Coat your hands lightly with oil and shape the cookie dough into two 5-inch logs. Wrap logs in plastic wrap and freeze 1–2 hours or until firm.

6. Preheat oven to 350 degrees.

7. Coat baking sheet(s) with cooking spray.

8. Unwrap frozen logs and slice into approximately 24 rounds (about 1/4-inch thick). Place the rounds on the baking sheet 1-inch apart.*

> *****
> You can store the dough in the freezer for up to a week, cutting and baking when the desire for warm cookies strikes.

9. Bake on the center rack for 8–9 minutes then remove from sheet. Note: Cookies should be soft. (If cookies are difficult to remove from the sheet, allow them to cool on the sheet for 30 seconds before removing.)

10. Eat warm or allow cookies to cool on a rack.

Super Sexy Me

perfect rose petal sorbet

recipe by Pat Rabin of Chillingsworth Restaurant
vegetarian
makes 4 servings

I call this sorbet "perfect" because when I first tasted it, my first thought was, "I want to eat this at my wedding." Pat, whose husband Nitzi contributed a recipe to *Fork Me,* makes it with the phenomenally fragrant roses in her garden. A subtly sweet, delicately floral sorbet, it can be used as a palate cleanser between courses, as a snack or guilt-free dessert. Although she loves making this ultra-romantic sorbet for special occasions, Pat warns that it requires the most fragrant roses possible to develop a deep, irresistible flavor.

1. Wash rose petals in a strainer.

2. Combine the sugar and water in a saucepan. Bring to a boil then boil for 5–7 minutes until it thickens to a syrup.

3. Remove sugar syrup from heat and add rose petals. Add the lemon juice and allow mixture to steep at least 6 hours or overnight in a cool place.

4. After the mixture has steeped, strain out rose petals then taste sorbet base. If it does not have a strong enough rose flavor, add the rose water. (This will depend on the fragrancy of the roses.) Chill the base in refrigerator for at least 2 hours before making the sorbet.

2 c organic rose petals, lightly packed, (for best color, use pink, red or a combination of colors)

1 c granulated sugar

2 c water

1 tbsp lemon juice

1/8 tsp rose water, (optional)

5. Add the base to an ice cream maker and make according to manufacturer instructions. If you do not have an ice cream maker, use the base to make a granita by pouring the base into a 9"x 13" metal pan and place in the freezer. Scrape the mixture with a fork every half hour to prevent it from freezing in one block. Repeat this process every half hour until no liquid remains, about 2–3 hours.

~6~
Quickies

I am a firm believer in eating well even when you don't have the time (or desire) to cook. In this chapter, I've shared a few of my favorite "busy day" recipes. After all, even if you just have time for a quickie, it should be delicious.

pick-me-up breakfast parfait

vegetarian

makes 1 parfait

You really have no excuse to skip breakfast with a recipe this simple. And your libido is going to thank you for packing the most important meal of the day with super-ingredients like blueberries and yogurt.

1/2 c your favorite fruit

1/2 c blueberries

1/2 c plain, Greek-style yogurt

2 tbsp your favorite granola or muesli

1. Cut fruit of your choice (strawberries, raspberries, blackberries, peaches, pears, apricots, mangos or figs recommended), and toss with blueberries.

2. Put 1/2 cup fruit at the bottom of a parfait cup or small bowl.

3. Add 1/4 cup yogurt, spreading to cover fruit, and 1 tbsp granola or muesli.

4. Top with remaining fruit, then cover with yogurt. Sprinkle with remaining granola or muesli.

fresh corn soup

makes 4 servings as appetizer or 2 for main course

When I first learned about kefir, the secret to this soup's creamy texture and distinctive flavor, I was amazed to discover that not only is it a complete protein (and one of the most easily digestible), it does all sorts of great things for the body. For the optimal flavor, try to get the freshest corn possible. The sweet, succulent taste farm fresh corn brings to the dish will astonish you.

1. Cut corn from cob and reserve both corn and cobs.

2. Heat oil in a stock pot over medium-high heat. Saute onion for 2 minutes. Add chicken stock and bring to a boil. Turn heat down to simmer and add corn, cobs, cumin, coriander and salt. Simmer for 15 minutes.

3. Turn off heat. Remove 2 tbsp of corn from the pot and set aside. Remove cobs and pour the remaining soup into the blender. Blend until smooth.

4. Stir in kefir, reserved corn kernels and (optional) chives. Season with additional salt to taste.

5. Serve immediately or chill at least 2 hours for a cold soup.

2 ears corn plus cobs
2 tsp canola oil
1 sm onion, chopped
1 3/4 c chicken stock
1/8 tsp cumin
1/4 tsp coriander
1/2 tsp salt
3/4 c kefir
1 tsp fresh chives, finely chopped, (optional)
salt and pepper to taste

steamy artichokes skinny dipping in honey

makes 2 servings

Steamed artichokes are typically served with a creamy, calorie-laden dip. But you don't need all that fat. In fact, dips usually mask the artichoke's true flavor. So instead, I've paired artichokes with a touch of honey, the nectar of Aphrodite, to augment their herbal flavors with an all-natural sweetness.

2 artichokes
2–3 tbsp honey

1. Fill a stock pot with approximately 1-inch of water. Cover the pot and bring the water to a boil, then turn the temperature down to low, keeping the pot covered.

2. Clean artichokes and cut the tops off so that if you turn them upside down, they will sit flat. Trim—but don't cut off—the stem. (Many people cut the stem off but this is one of the meatiest parts of the artichoke.) Then trim off any sharp points on the ends of leaves.

3. Put the artichokes in the pot, stems facing up, so they sit flat, and steam for 20–30 minutes, until the leaves pull off easily. If the water runs low, add a small, additional amount.*

4. Transfer artichokes to a serving plate and serve with the honey for dipping.

> *****
> If you're in a rush, you can more quickly steam the artichokes in the microwave. Just be prepared for the outer leaves to discolor.

afternoon delight crab salad

makes 2 servings

Sometimes a simple salad fits the bill. The trick is to find the combination of ingredients that keeps the dish light but makes it satisfying. For me, crab salad with crunchy apples, salty bursts of capers and the creamy texture of avocados does the job. The crab mixture also works well as a dip. Just mash the avocado and blend it in to give the dip a smooth texture and serve with pita chips, page 109, or raw veggies and fruits.

1. In a small mixing bowl, combine crab, apple, celery, onion, capers, cream cheese and Dijon, mixing thoroughly.
2. Season with salt then gently fold in chives.
3. Evenly divide the greens between 2 plates. Top with the crab and garnish plates with the avocado. Squeeze fresh lemon juice over both salads before serving.

5 oz crab meat or a 6 oz can of crab, drained

1/2 crisp, red apple, (such as a Fuji or Braeburn), cored, (not peeled), and finely chopped

1 tbsp celery, finely chopped

1 tbsp sweet onion, (such as Vidalia), finely chopped

1 1/2 tsp capers, drained

1 1/2 tbsp cream cheese, softened

1 tsp Dijon mustard

1/4 tsp salt

1 tsp fresh chives, minced

2 c baby greens

1/2 avocado, thinly sliced

wedge of fresh lemon

vegetarian drunken meatballs *(albondigas)*

vegetarian

makes 4 servings

Meatballs are a popular part of Spanish tapas. My version uses another popular Spanish tradition: wine. Because I layer the meatballs with additional flavors, I think its fine to use ready-made. To keep this super-quick appetizer light, I buy veggie meatballs (which tend to be more flavorful and won't slow you down digesting all that fat). You can, of course, use any kind of meatball you like but, just for me, promise you'll go veggie at least once.

2 tsp olive oil

1 spanish onion, roughly chopped

16 frozen vegetarian meatballs*

1 c dry white wine

1 tbsp flat leaf parsley, finely chopped

1. Over medium heat, coat the bottom of a small stock pan with oil. Sauté the onion until soft, about 2 minutes.

2. Add the meatballs to the pot and sauté until brown on at least 2 sides (an additional 2 or 3 minutes).

3. Add white wine and turn temperature to low. Simmer, covered, for 15 minutes.

4. Remove from heat and transfer meatballs and onions to a serving dish with a slotted spoon. (Meatballs will be very moist. Move them gently to ensure you don't wind up with a pile of ground soy.)

5. Sprinkle parsley over meatballs as a garnish.

*

The recipe also works with turkey, pork and beef meatballs but I love the clean flavor and health benefits of the soy variety.

Remaining liquid can be discarded or used as a sauce for simple baked or seared fish.

Since Albondigas is a Spanish tradition, try simmering the meatballs in a dry, Spanish white wine, like an Albariño, then enjoy the rest of the bottle as your effort's reward.

easy vegan carrot top pesto

vegetarian

serves 4–6 when used as a pasta topping

I like to buy my carrots at the farmers' market, where they come fully intact with their tops of glorious greens. I know that the tops are not only edible but extremely nutritious. I could just never figure out what to do with them. Saddened by throwing all the greens in the compost bin week after week, I finally came up with this pesto recipe. And since we know that walnuts, garlic and olive oil are all great for the libido, I figured it was not only a practical recipe but a great one for the book! The classic way to use this sauce is as a pasta topping. I make mine with linguine, which means "little tongues" (appropriate). But I also use it as a dip for veggies, salad dressing and spread for bread.

1. Toast walnuts in pan or oven until golden. Set aside.

2. Heat 1 tbsp olive oil over medium heat. Saute the onions in the pan until soft. Add garlic and saute an additional minute before stirring in the carrot tops and a pinch of smoked salt. Cook until carrot tops wilt, about 1 minute.

3. Transfer carrot top mixture to a blender, adding toasted walnuts and 1 tbsp water. Blend, adding olive oil in a slow stream until mixture becomes a coarse paste (the texture of pesto). You may not need all the olive oil or you may need additional.

1/4 c unsalted walnuts

1 tbsp + 1/4 c olive oil

1 tbsp sweet onion, roughly chopped

1 clove garlic, roughly chopped

1 bunch carrot tops, thoroughly washed and roughly chopped*

smoked salt to taste

1 tbsp water

black pepper, (optional)

1 lb whole wheat linguine

easy vegan carrot top pesto

chocolate kissed
white bean chili,
pg 50

below: pomegranate
roasted pork loin
with quinoa and
sexy veg, pg 62

left: sensual spices; *below:* herb massaged london broil with simple grilled asparagus, pg 80

4. Season with additional smoked salt to taste. If you like a little heat, try adding in a touch of freshly ground black pepper. Set aside while you prepare the pasta.

5. Make pasta according to package instructions, cooking to al dente.

6. Drain pasta and toss with the pesto. Serve immediately. Alternatively, serve the pesto at room temperature as a dipping sauce or refrigerate and use as a salad dressing.

stovetop sous vide salmon on a bed of apricots and fennel

makes 4 servings

Sous vide, French for "under vacuum," is a cooking method gaining popularity in the "molecular gastronomy," fine dining craze. While true sous vide cooking requires an expensive piece of equipment called a thermal circulator, there is a way to take the core idea of sous vide cooking (slowly poaching a protein—in this case fish—in a vacuum sealed bag to lock in moisture and flavor) and use the concept at home in a low-tech guise. (You will not quite get the same effect as you would from a thermal circulator because this piece of equipment actually stirs the water, guaranteeing even cooking. But I think, with salmon, anyway, the results of our method are sufficiently satisfying and make a fine introduction to this low-fat, high snob-appeal style of cooking.)

I use a small vacuum sealer for this recipe—if you are looking for a gadget worth an investment, this is definitely one to consider; a vacuum sealer has a multitude of uses. But you can get almost the same effect from tight plastic wrap sealing.

It may seem strange that I've chosen a dish using slow poaching as a "quickie" but I think the finished dish's complexity of flavor and level of presentation offer pretty fabulous return on investment for the amount of prep time. And since your hands are free while the fish poaches, the possibility of a predinner quickie isn't out of the question!

12 oz wild salmon, 1/2–3/4-inch thickness

salt and pepper to taste

1 garlic clove, peeled and sliced

1 small lemon, sliced into rounds

1 fennel bulb

1/2 c Vidalia or other sweet onion

6 dried apricots

1 tbsp lemon zest

2 tsp grape seed or other neutral oil

2 tbsp apple cider vinegar

4 tsp salmon roe, (or more if desired)

1. Place a pot of water over a burner and heat to 113 degrees, checking constantly with a thermometer.

2. Season salmon with salt and pepper and place in a vacuum sealer bag with the garlic and lemon. Vacuum seal the bag shut. (If you do not own a vacuum sealer, tightly wrap salmon, garlic and lemon in a layer of plastic wrap. Prick the plastic wrap and press out any air. Cut a second piece of plastic wrap that is at least twice the length of the fish. Wrap the parcel in the second piece of plastic wrap so that the ends will fold over the opposite sides of the first piece of plastic wrap. This is to help ensure the package stays watertight. Pull wrap as tightly as you can before sealing ends.

3. Submerge fish parcel in the 113-degree water.

4. Get a cup of ice and keep it within reach while you monitor the water temperature. If temperature gets above 120 degrees, drop ice into water, one cube at a time until temperature returns to 113 degrees (but not below). Cook, monitoring in this fashion for 15–20 minutes, depending on thickness of salmon fillets. (The thicker the steak, the longer it should cook. If you like your fish on the rare side, cook for less minutes. If you prefer your fish cooked through, cook for the full poaching time.)

5. Take packet from water and remove fish, discarding garlic and lemon.

for the fennel-apricot slaw:

1. Using a food processor or mandolin, shave fennel and onion into paper-thin slices, reserving the dill-like fennel tops (fronds).

2. Finely chop apricots and mix in a bowl with fennel and onions. Add lemon zest, oil and vinegar and toss until fennel is thoroughly coated.

3. Add in 1 tbsp of fennel fronds for color and season with salt and pepper to taste. (Slaw can be made a day in advance, but step 3 should be reserved until serving.)

To serve:

Place 1/4 of the slaw on each of 2 plates (sprinkle with fronds and season with salt and pepper if this was not done in advance). Top with 3 oz salmon and garnish each with 1 tsp salmon roe.

Salmon with Pinot Noir is a much-loved pairing among the food and wine "elite." I recommend trying the combination, especially since Pinot Noir has some of the highest levels of resveratrol of all wines. (For more on resveratrol, see Chapter 8, *Don't Whine— Wine!*)

Store remaining fish, roe and slaw in separate containers and plate at the last minute. Leftover fish can be served cold, or gently rewarmed before serving.

champagne with a rose water kiss

makes 2 drinks

This is one of my simplest tricks for delivering a complex cocktail. Sparkling wine is already layered with interesting attributes from its icy chill to its effervescence and bright array of flavors. By adding just a trace of rose water, you're emphasizing the Champagne's aphrodisiac attributes while allowing the wine's natural flavors to still shine.

2–4 drops rose water

10 oz Champagne or sparkling wine

1. Place 1–2 drops rose water into each of 2 Champagne flutes. (For added ease, use an eye dropper.)

2. Top each with 5 oz Champagne or sparkling wine.

3. Drink.

speedy cmp fondue
(chocolate-marshmallow-peanut)

serves 2

My great grandmother Amy (for whom I was named) owned an ice cream parlor. One of her most popular items was the CMP sundae (chocolate, marshmallow and peanuts). In this recipe, I've eliminated the ice cream and have gone straight for the good stuff. (I've also layered the chocolate flavor with a healthy dose of cacao nibs—nibs are the chocolate at its most pure and are loaded with antioxidants as well as a terrific, crunchy texture.) By turning the CMP into a fondue, it becomes an interactive dish, one that is fun for sharing, feeding and foreplay.

1. Put peanuts in a shallow bowl.

2. In a double boiler over hot (not boiling) water, melt butter. Stir in chocolate and corn syrup, stirring constantly until melted.

3. Remove from heat and add vanilla and nibs.

4. Dip marshmallows first in the chocolate, then roll in the peanuts. Eat immediately to enjoy the melty, crunchy combo.

If you aren't planning to serve immediately, transfer chocolate to a fondue pot to keep warm.

Variation: Place 1/2 fresh strawberry and 1 mini marshmallow on a toothpick or skewer. Dip in chocolate and peanuts for a juicy, summery variation on the dessert.

---

*
If you are trying to watch your sodium intake, use unsalted peanuts and sprinkle them with a pinch of coarse sea salt.

---

2 tbsp roasted, salted peanuts, finely chopped*

1 tbsp butter

1/4 c dark chocolate chips

1 tsp light corn syrup

1/2 tsp vanilla

2 tsp cacao nibs**

8 marshmallows

**
Cacao nibs can be found in baking supply stores, gourmet grocers and online.

sensual strawberry-apple bread pudding

recipe by Chrysta Wilson, author of the bestselling cookbook
Kiss My Bundt: recipes from the
award-winning bakery
makes 8 servings

2 c (approx) French
bread, chopped

3 eggs

1 c unsweetened
soymilk

4 oz chevre, (soft goat
cheese)

3/4 c white sugar

1 bottle Cava or Brut
Sparkling Wine

1 medium gala apple,
cubed*

1/2 c strawberries,
thinly sliced*

---

*

Depending on the
season, you can
swap out the apples
and strawberries for
peaches, figs or
mangoes. You can
also replace the
strawberry with
raspberry. Chrysta
makes a version
that's all apple and
tops it with caramel
sauce.

One night Chrysta, who is not only my favorite cake baker but has become a good friend, was doing a mock Iron Chef challenge in my kitchen with me and a few friends. Presented with farm fresh eggs and a log of chevre as her "secret ingredients" and amply fueled on Cava, Chrysta came up with this unbelievably easy, reasonably healthy and ridiculously tasty bread pudding recipe.

1. Preheat oven to 350 degrees.

2. Coat a small baking dish with canola oil.

3. Chop baguette into bite-sized pieces.

4. In a large mixing bowl, whisk eggs. Add in soymilk, chevre, sugar and 1/2 cup Cava to make a custard.

5. Put bread, apples and strawberries in an oiled, 9"x 13" baking dish, pouring the custard over the top.

6. Let the bread pudding stand for 10 minutes while you drink the rest of the Cava.

7. Bake for 25–30 minutes or until custard is set.

Serve with additional Cava.

~7~
Nibbles, Bites and Afternoon Delights

I'm a snacker. I've always been a snacker. But about 10 years ago I began suffering from bouts of low blood sugar. The experience taught me how important snacking can be for keeping you energized, focused and in a good mood. All of these things are important elements to becoming a successful seductress, seductor or seductee! And because I think a snack can be just as sensual as a meal, I've layered this chapter's recipes with irresistible aphrodisiac ingredients.

bikini bread

vegetarian
makes 1 loaf

As a child, I thought a two-piece bathing suit was called a zucchini. Even though I no longer confuse my bikini with a summer squash, I still think the two have something in common. Made with whole wheat flour, a dose of veggies and healthy walnuts, this sweet can actually help keep you in bikini shape. I like to serve bikini bread as an alternative to a muffin or scone or as a pick-me-up for the afternoon slump.

1 1/2 c whole wheat flour

1/2 tsp salt

1/4 tsp baking soda

1/4 tsp baking powder

2 tsp cinnamon

2 eggs, room temperature

1 c sugar

1/2 c vegetable oil

1 1/2 tsp vanilla

1 c zucchini, grated

1/2 chopped walnuts, (optional)

1. Preheat oven to 350 degrees (325 degrees if using a glass loaf pan).

2. Sift together flour, salt, baking soda, baking powder and cinnamon. Set aside.

3. Using an electric mixer, beat eggs on medium speed for 2 minutes.

4. Add sugar, oil and vanilla and beat for an additional 2 minutes then mix in zucchini.

5. Turn mixer speed to low and add in the flour mixture, about 1/2 cup at a time, mixing until flour is just combined. Fold in (optional) walnuts.*

   *
   Batter can be made up to 24 hours in advance.

6. Pour batter into a loaf pan that has been thoroughly greased and floured and bake until an inserted toothpick or cake tester comes out clean, about 50–55 minutes.

7. Remove from pan immediately and cool on a wire rack.

Nibbles, Bites and Afternoon Delights

naughty girl grilled cherries

vegetarian

makes 4 servings

To me, cherries are uber-naughty-plump, perfectly proportioned and slut red in color. They're like the red, patent leather pumps of fruit. This recipe gives cherries a new spin. Grilling caramelizes a bit of their sugar and, served warm, their sweet juices positively ooze in a most enticing way. The pinch of curry, crunch of nuts and zing of salt takes cherries to a whole new level of sensuality.

1. Heat grill to medium-high.

2. Using a grill basket, grill cherries for 3 minutes per side.

3. Remove from grill and sprinkle with curry powder, pistachios and salt. Allow cherries to cool 5 minutes before eating. (Straight off the grill, the fruit's caramelized sugar can burn your mouth. In this instance, patience is a virtue!)

12 whole Bing or other black cherry

1/4 tsp curry powder

2 tsp roasted, unsalted pistachio nuts, chopped

pinch salt

surprise someone soybean dip

vegetarian

makes 4 servings

You typically see soybeans (edamame) in Japanese restaurants (those little snacks served in the pod). But you can also buy shelled soybeans in the freezer section of many grocery and health food stores. Keep a bag handy to make this quick dip for last minute guests, or as a light snack on nights when you're too tired to cook. You can also use it as a sandwich spread (see the green grilled cheese on the next page) or serve it to your kids with a bowl of chips to sneak some veggies into their diets. No one will believe that this dip is made from soybeans—or that it's full of fantastic nutrients.

1 c steamed soybeans, (edamame)

1/4 c fresh spinach leaves, roughly chopped

1/4 tsp garlic, (approx 1/2 clove), minced

1 tbsp lemon juice

2 tsp olive oil

1/2 c vegetable stock

1/2 tsp dry mustard

salt and white pepper to taste

1. Put ingredients in a blender and purée until smooth.

2. Season with salt and pepper before serving.

3. Serve as a dip with vegetables, chips or thyme-sprinkled whole wheat pita chips (page 109), or use as a spread on sandwiches.

Dip can be kept, refrigerated, for up to 5 days.

green grilled cheese for lovers

makes 1 sandwich

1. Thinly spread both sides of bread with butter. (I prefer a really hearty whole grain.)

2. Heat a nonstick pan over medium heat. Toast one side of the bread to golden brown, flip the bread and remove it from the pan.

3. Spread the toasted side of the bread with the soybean dip and sprinkle with the cheese.

4. Return the sandwich to the pan, uncooked side down and cook to a golden brown.

5. Put the sandwich under the broiler until the cheese starts to bubble.

1 slice your favorite sandwich bread

1–2 tsp butter

1 tbsp soybean dip, (previous page)

2 tbsp your favorite cheese, grated

thyme tickled whole wheat pita chips

vegetarian

makes 4 servings

This is my quick alternative to the processed snacks sold in grocery stores. The thyme leaves combined with earthy, whole wheat take snacking to a new level. Try them with anything from my soybean dip (page 107), to guacamole, herbed chevre and even as croutons on my crab salad (page 94).

2 whole wheat pitas
olive oil for brushing
2 tsp fresh thyme
   leaves

1. Preheat oven to 350 degrees.

2. Using a pastry brush, brush both sides of each pita with olive oil.

3. Sprinkle the tops of the pitas with the thyme leaves, pressing them down slightly, into the oil.*

4. Cut each pita into 6 triangles and arrange the triangles on a baking sheet.

5. Bake until the pitas crisp, 12–16 minutes, depending on your oven and the thickness of the pitas. (If you like your pitas crisp on the edges with softness in the middle, cook for a shorter period of time. If you like them completely crunchy, cook longer but check frequently to avoid burning.)

*
If you like your snacks a little salty, you can sprinkle the tops with a pinch of coarse sea salt when you add the thyme.

one & only salad dressing

makes 4–6 servings

Not only is this the perfect dressing for your one and only but this is the one and only vinaigrette I ever make. I change it up a little every time. Sometimes I add a little balsamic vinegar and/or a pinch of Herbes de Provence. And sometimes I use smoked salt. It is the perfect dressing for anyone counting calories because it incorporates only just enough oil to cling to the lettuce leaves and such intensity of flavor that you need only use splash.

1. Finely mince shallot and put it, along with the red wine vinegar, Dijon and rosemary into a small mixing bowl.

2. Using a wire whisk, slowly whisk in the olive oil, using just enough to give the dressing a glossy shine and vinaigrette consistency.

3. Season with salt and pepper to taste.

1/2 medium shallot
2 tbsp red wine vinegar
1 tbsp Dijon mustard
1 pinch dried rosemary
1–2 tsp fruity olive oil
salt and pepper to taste

feta & basil stuffed mushrooms

vegetarian

makes 4 servings

Nobody will ever guess that the stuffing in these mushrooms is half tofu. The thing about tofu is that it tends to take on the flavor of whatever is cooked with it, so here, the tofu pretty much tastes like feta. Yet you're getting all of tofu's health benefits, including protein and estrogen. But trust me, none of that will matter after just one tempting bite!

12 large or "stuffing" white mushroom caps

1 tsp olive oil

1/4 c yellow onion, finely chopped

1 garlic clove, minced

1/2 c light tofu

1/4 tsp mustard powder

1 tsp Worcestershire sauce

1/4 tsp salt

1/4 tsp black pepper

1/3 c fat free feta

1/4 c fresh baby spinach, roughly chopped

1 tbsp fresh basil, minced

2 tbsp panko, (Japanese breadcrumbs)

1. Preheat oven to 350 degrees.

2. Wash mushrooms and remove stems. Place mushrooms stem-side down in a shallow baking dish coated with cooking spray. Cook for 10 minutes. Remove any excess liquid from the baking dish and set aside.

3. In a nonstick sauté pan, heat olive oil. Sauté the onions until soft, about 2 minutes. Add in garlic, tofu, mustard powder, Worcestershire sauce, salt and pepper and cook for an additional 2 minutes.

4. Add in feta, spinach and basil and remove pan from heat.

5. Stir in panko.

6. Turn mushrooms over so that the stuffing side is up then stuff the mushrooms.

7. Cook for 15 minutes or until tender and stuffing is slightly golden.

Nibbles, Bites and Afternoon Delights

mind bending blue cheese walnut brittle

vegetarian

makes 12–14 servings

From its name, I realize this combination sounds a little crazy. But it just might be my favorite recipe in the entire book. I love the earthy flavor that the walnuts, thyme and blue cheese add to what I think is often an overly sweet snack. Most brittle recipes start with water and allow it to evaporate through the cooking process. But I prefer the straightforward method in which the sugar simply melts in the pan like magic. Although the process requires faithful attention, making this recipe is incredibly fun. You may find it takes a couple of tries to get the technique down, but the results are so worth it.

1. Chop the thyme leaves to release some of their oil.

2. In a small mixing bowl, toss together the walnuts, blue cheese and thyme until walnuts are thoroughly coated with cheese and no visible blue cheese crumbles remain. Set aside.

3. Line a baking sheet with wax paper or, ideally, a silicone baking mat. If using wax paper, brush the surface of the wax paper with oil. Lay an identical-sized piece of wax paper (or silicone mat) on the counter and brush with oil. (While wax paper can stick, silicone mats will lift right off the finished brittle.)

4. Heat a heavy saucepan over high heat. When pan is hot, sprinkle in just enough of the sugar to coat the bottom of the pan and begin to stir the sugar. Sugar will start to melt into a caramel.

1 tsp fresh thyme leaves

1 1/4 c roasted, unsalted walnuts, coarsely chopped*

1/4 c blue cheese, crumbled

oil for brushing

2 c granulated sugar

1/2 tsp coarse salt

5. Turn temperature down to medium and sprinkle in more sugar, 3 tbsp at a time, stirring. Continue adding sugar at this rate as the hot sugar melts. If the color of the mixture starts to get any darker than light amber, remove the pan from the heat for a few seconds to allow it to cool.

6. Once you've used half of the sugar, begin adding sugar to the mixture at a rate of 1/3 cup at a time. Continue to stir and monitor the color. You do not want the sugar to get too dark.

7. When all the sugar has been incorporated, turn heat to low and add the walnut mixture, stirring until incorporated.

8. Quickly transfer brittle from the pan to the lined baking sheet. Be careful not to touch the hot brittle, it will burn. Cover the brittle with the second sheet of wax paper (oil side down) or silicone mat. Using a rolling pin, roll brittle out to about a 1/4-inch to 1/3-inch thickness.

9. Allow brittle to cool for about 5–8 minutes, until top layer of wax paper pulls back easily, but surface of the brittle is still a little sticky. Sprinkle the top with the salt then replace the wax paper. Allow the brittle to cool completely before removing both sheets of wax paper and breaking it into pieces.

Store brittle in an airtight container.

***

*

Unsalted walnuts can be found in the baking section of most grocery stores. Look for "baking pieces" to get a prechopped product.

Nibbles, Bites and Afternoon Delights

susan feniger's sexy banana fritters with coconut kaya jam

recipe by Chef Susan Feniger of STREET restaurant
and Border Grill
makes 6–8 servings

Since both coconut and banana are aphrodisiac, we thought this would make a great contribution. We use Kaya a great deal at my restaurant, STREET, and numerous diners have commented that they wish they could rub the jam all over their body! So, my sense is that, beyond the known aphrodisiacs, there is something about this recipe that makes it is a very sensual dish.

—Chef Susan Feniger

First, make your Coconut Kaya Jam so it has time to cool and thicken. This can be done up to 3 days in advance but should be made at least 2 hours before the fritters.

1. In a small saucepan, mix together the coconut milk and 1/3 cup sugar.

2. Place the pandan and salt into the pot with the coconut/sugar mixture. Bring to a boil, pushing down the pandan leaves into the milk as they cook and soften.

3. When the liquid boils, turn off the heat and steep for 20 minutes, or until the pandan is cool enough to handle with your bare hands.

For the Coconut Kaya Jam:
2/3 c coconut milk, stirred well

2/3 c granulated sugar

6 pandan leaves, washed and tied into a knot*

pinch kosher salt

2 eggs

2 egg yolks

4. Pull out the pandan leaves and squeeze them into the coconut mixture to extract as much flavor and liquid as possible. Throw out the leaves and set the liquid aside.

5. Whisk together the eggs, yolks and remaining 1/3 cup sugar in a stainless steel mixing bowl.

6. Slowly whisk in the coconut mixture and place the bowl over a saucepan of lightly simmering water to make a double boiler.

7. Cook gently, stirring continually with a rubber spatula, until the mixture thickens. This takes approximately 15 to 20 minutes. It will seem like a long time before you see any results, but then the moment the mixture starts to set, the jam becomes easy to overcook. So be careful if your tendency is to walk away. The texture should be that of a thick custard consistency.

8. When finished, spread the jam into a clean container and place in the refrigerator to cool.

Once your Kaya Jam is made, the rest of the recipe takes very little time.

To fry the bananas:

1. Whisk together the rice flour, all-purpose flour, sugar, sesame seeds and salt. Slowly whisk in the soda water to create the consistency of a loose pancake batter. Set aside.

2. Fill the pan with vegetable oil so that the oil reaches halfway up the sides. A low, wide pan with 3-inch sides or a wok works best. Remember, the oil will expand and rise as it heats.

3. Heat the oil on medium heat for approximately 4 to 5 minutes, or until a test drop of batter floats immediately when dropped into the oil.

4. Peel the bananas and cut lengthwise into thin slices, about 4 per banana. If using large bananas, cut them horizontally in half as well.

5. Dip each slice in the batter and fry 2 to 3 minutes on each side or until golden brown, flipping once. Remove fritters from the oil and drain on a plate lined with paper towels.

For the batter:
1/3 c rice flour

3/4 c all-purpose flour

1 1/2 tbsp granulated sugar

4 tbsp toasted sesame seeds

1/2 tsp kosher salt

1 c soda water

4 ripe bananas

Serve immediately with a dipping bowl of the Kaya Jam.

If there is leftover jam, try spreading it on toast for a slightly exotic breakfast treat.

~8~
Don't Whine—
Wine!

I firmly believe there's a place for alcohol in the games of romance. (As if you hadn't already picked up on this from my recipe chapters.) Of course, every time I mention alcohol in an interview on aphrodisiac foods, some smarty pants always has to point out that alcohol, in the words of William Shakespeare, "provokes the desire but inhibits the performance." And yes, it can have that effect when consumed recklessly. But since this book is all about listening to and making your body happy, I'm entrusting you to know your limits and indulge in the first only to the point where it *enhances*, not inhibits, the other.

If you still feel unsure about mixing alcohol and libido my best advice to you is rather than whine, always choose wine. (I always enjoy a good rule of thumb delivered in rhyme.) Wine is lower in alcohol than spirits, making it easier to enjoy without crossing that line of no return and it won't bloat you like beer. Since this book is all about the foods of love, I should also add that wine is among the world's most romantic beverages. It is made by passionate people from fruits grown in some of the most beautiful locales on earth. Its flavor is a balance between nature and the skill of a winemaker, a culinary artisan as well-trained and creative as a chef.

Wine and Health

Many doctors recommend a glass of wine (or two) a day for the heart. But what most MD's don't mention is that wine can also be great for your romantic life. The antioxidants in wine not only help to protect the heart but, because they help stop free radicals, it is believed that they also minimize the impact of aging. That's right, wine can help keep you looking your most youthful and feeling your most sexy!

Research on the topic is ever evolving but it is thought that certain types of red wine grapes offer the body the greatest concentration of antioxidants. Wines made from Pinot Noir as well as two more unusual grapes, Muscadine and Tannat, are promoted as offering the greatest antioxidant benefit. But every red wine offers some degree of reward. (Interestingly, the benefit varies somewhat by the region in which the grapes are grown as well as the vintage.)

It was recently discovered, to my great glee, that Champagnes and other Sparkling Wines made with the inclusion of red grapes (very often Pinot Noir) also offer both the same heart and anti-aging benefits as red wine.

White Wine—the Health Powerhouse

Never fear white wine drinkers! As with all types of alcohol, white wine is beneficial for raising good cholesterol. And although all the talk in the news tends to be about red wine and its high concentration of antioxidants, several university studies have concluded that the antioxidants found in grape pulp, although different than those found in the skin, are equally beneficial to heart health.

Several academic papers have, in fact, declared the antioxidants in white wine superior to those in red wines. While examining white wines in depth, Dr. Gordon Troup of Monash University in Melbourne, Australia found that the smaller size of the molecules in white wine made them easier to absorb and therefore more effective than red wine antioxidants. Additional studies have found white wine more effective than other types of alcohol in reducing blood pressure. Go Riesling!

The Scent of Seduction

And while it takes time for wine to produce anti-aging effects on the body, the scent of wine plays a more immediate role in games of love. Australian vintner and researcher, the late Dr. Max Lake (a mentor of mine who is sorely missed), discovered that the scents of certain wines replicate the aromas of pheromones.

Attraction pheromones are those little scent receptors helping to signal magnetism in the brain. Now, I'm not saying that a pheromone-laced wine will land you a lover totally out of your league, but they certainly can help get your partner (and you) in the mood if your plans include seduction.

The best-known pheromonal scent is that earthy, musky, faintly truffle-like note found in many Pinot Noirs. This irresistible aroma is said to replicate that of the male pheromone androstenone. The scent is found in wines beyond Pinot but somehow this delicate grape tends to deliver this musky goodness with the most finesse. If Pinot isn't your thing, Dr. Lake recommends looking for the arousing aroma of cedar in some common wine styles and varietals, including Bordeaux blends and Cabernet Sauvignons, as well as some Shiraz.

There is a line of thought that it is the process of aging wine in new oak that produces the androstenone-like aromas. It makes sense, considering that the scent of cedar and its close cousin sandalwood, which Dr. Lake attests closely resemble androstenone, develop in the wine during barrel aging. This would also help explain why some Chardonnays elicit an aphrodisiac response in women. And it certainly sheds an interesting new light on the American obsession with big, oaky wines!

But according to Dr. Lake's research, there are more delicate wine aromas that also trigger an aphrodisiac response. Dr. Lake found that a certain yeasty note in Champagnes and Sparkling Wines is reminiscent of a female pheromone. The scent is most often found in sophisticated Blanc de Blancs but this bread dough-like note can also be found in Brut-style bubbly. In addition, the sensual, sweaty aromas in Riesling and the musky notes of many Chardonnays also replicate pheromone scents.

Cooking with Wine

I, for one, am an enthusiast of cooking with wine. And by that I mean cooking with a glass of wine in hand. Wine to me is a magical drink.

I still remember my first sip. My parents took my brother and I on a road trip down the Pacific Northwest coast into the California Bay Area. Somewhere around Mendocino, I guess the parents got inspired by the local wine fever and offered me a taste at dinner. Sorry for outing you, Mom and Dad, but that first sip was, for me, a game changer. (It was Jekel Riesling by the way. No surprise that to this day Riesling remains my favorite grape.)

The love affair continued from that day forward. My first job after college was in the tasting room at Ferrari Carano winery in Sonoma County's Dry Creek Valley and by 25 I had my first wine article published on the *New York Times* wine website.

I tell you this so that I don't come off as a total lush when I say that enjoying a glass of wine while cooking is an almost essential part of preparing a meal for me.

A little wine (and to be honest I rarely imbibe in more than half a glass when working with fire and knives) can serve as a muscle relaxant, helping to ease not only the string of knots running across my shoulder blades but also release some tension in the mind. Believe it or not, I find a few sips of wine makes concentrating on a recipe easier by dimming the endless ping-pong of thoughts bouncing around in my head.

I also believe that a few sips of wine while cooking helps to inject a bit of love into the meal. (And how can you serve a meal of seduction that hasn't been cooked with love?)

I generally sip the wine I'll be serving with dinner as I cook. Although I am not a huge proponent of worrying about pairing your wine with your meal, sipping the wine you're serving can help you to tweak the seasonings as you go, sort of tuning the dish to the flavors you're tasting in the wine to really take the experience of the meal to another level.

As for what wine to use in cooking, I generally use the same wine I'm drinking, if it's something everyday. Although the popular advice is to ALWAYS use the wine you plan to serve in your cooking, some wines are simply too special as far as I'm concerned! It isn't necessary to deglaze a pan with that precious Lafite, (in fact, I'd probably hunt you down if you did). Just promise me you won't ever use that horrible stuff sold in the grocery store as "cooking wine." My general rule on this is: if you wouldn't drink it, neither should your pot!

~9~
Amy's Dictionary of Desire

Foods of Desire—*Some of my favorite aphrodisiac foods include, but are not limited to:*

Apples—The symbol of temptation—and of health— apples are the true emblem of the aphrodisiac world. But apples' powers of temptation are not in the looks department alone. Their antioxidants fight aging and the fruit's skin offers much-needed fiber. (An aphrodisiac truth: regularity can be one of the keys to a happy relationship!)

Basil—The stimulating scent of basil is touted in the aromatherapy world for its ability to awaken the senses. In addition, little basil leaves pack a nutritional punch, offering the body beta carotene, vitamins A and C, as well as magnesium and manganese.

Blueberries—Low in calories and high in fiber, blueberries have one of the highest antioxidant levels among all fruits. And, according to health professor Mary Ellen Carnire, their nutritional makeup can also help to alleviate erectile malfunctions.

Buffalo—see Wild Game

Champagne (and other sparkling wines)—Champagne not only offers the heart health benefits of red wine but studies show that sparkling wine also supports the brain. From personal experience, I can tell you that bubbly brings an air of flirtation and festivity to any occasion and that the pearl-like strings bubbles hitting the bloodstream results in giddy abandon. For more on Champagne's allure, see Chapter 8, *Don't Whine—Wine!*

Cheese—Doctors say that cheese is great for the teeth because it lowers levels of bacteria in the mouth. Makes you want to kiss a cheese eater, doesn't it? Cheese also contains phenylethylamine, a naturally occurring chemical compound that acts as a sort of natural amphetamine. Researcher Dr. Max Lake found that the scent of triple cream cheeses replicated that of a female pheromone. (Who would have thought brie could bring excitement to your bedroom?)

Chile Peppers—One of the most talked-about aphrodisiacs of the plant world, chile has the ability to raise body temperature, make the tongue tingle and bring an alluring flush to the cheeks. Some researchers have even said that eating chiles can cause an all-out endorphin rush. (I don't know about you but this sounds like a much more appealing route than running a marathon for that natural high.)

Chocolate—It *is* true that chocolate contains chemical compounds with the potential for elevating mood, perking energy and warming things in the nether regions. But—I'm sorry to report—its been proven that an average-sized adult would have to consume more than 20 lbs of chocolate in one sitting to achieve such a hot rush. *(Diabetic coma, anyone?)* That being said, chocolate's caffeine-like properties can boost energy and the antioxidants in dark chocolate and cocoa can be beneficial in the fight against aging.

Cocoa—see *Chocolate*

Coffee—The aphrodisiac of adrenalin, coffee is an excellent aid for sparking amorous encounters. Coffee can also rev up metabolism and its been shown to aid concentration. Scientific studies have even proved that coffee can promote the production of dopamine, a neurotransmitter associated not only with pleasure but also cognition, memory and motivation.

Amy's Dictionary of Desire

Eggs—Because of their association with new life, eggs have been considered a symbol of fertility by nearly every culture enamored with aphrodisiacs. They provide the body with the protein needed for a long night of passion and offer vitamin E, selenium, iodine and vitamin B12—all of which are important to maintaining sexual health. Caviar, my favorite eggs of them all, also provides zinc, which is essential for blood flow.

Fennel—A good one for the ladies, fennel is high in plant estrogens. I love fennel for its subtly sweet anise flavor and crunch but its also rich in vitamin C, a good source of fiber and helps promote the antioxidant activity that keeps us young and fabulous.

Garlic—Garlic is a global cure-all as old as recorded time. It has been used to treat everything from sleep apnea to cancer. The ancient Greeks fed it to their athletes prior to Olympic competition for increased stamina—the kind of assistance we could all use, be we Olympians or common folk.

Ginger—Ginger is fantastic for warming up the body and the bedroom. It is effective in stimulating both the circulatory and digestive systems. We want that blood pumping!

Honey—An all-natural sweetener, honey is sexy just in its appearance (and the promise of playtime a little drizzle can spark). But it also offers the body boron, which helps us utilize estrogen. And, of course, a little taste can boost blood sugar and offer a bit of energy at a critical moment.

Mussels—In 2005, a group of researchers discovered that an amino acid in mussels directly raised sexual hormone levels—how's that for an aphrodisiac? A lean protein, mussels are also a good mood food, providing Omega-3's.

Mustard—We think of mustard as that yellow paste smeared on ham sandwiches but mustard seed is actually a sexual powerhouse that is rich in aphrodisiac history. Until modern times, monks were banned from eating mustard because of its aphrodisiac powers. Today, we know that mustard seeds offer several nutrients vital to sexual health, including selenium, magnesium, Omega-3's and zinc.

Nuts—Nuts are high in fiber and protein. They provide the body with vitamin E, also called the "sex vitamin." In addition, studies indicate that nuts have the potential to elevate serotonin levels, a bonus, feel-good effect.

Oysters—The old cliché is true, oysters are great for your sex life (unless you're allergic to bivalves). Yes, they're a good source of zinc and lean protein but thanks to recent research, we suspect that they could also promote sexual hormone production.

Peaches—Sweet, fuzzy peaches earned a folkloric rep as aphrodisiacs because, it was felt, their form resembled a curvaceous, female buttock. We're not so sure about the comparison but we do know that peaches are a good source of fiber, vitamin C, vitamin A and also offer some potassium and magnesium.

Pomegranate—A ruby red jewel of the Middle East, pomegranate was regaled as a culinary symbol of Aphrodite by the ancient Greeks. The fruit is one of the finest sources of antioxidants available. But its greatest promise of aphrodisiac power may be a study published in the *International Journal of Impotence Research*, which concluded that pomegranate juice has potential to treat erectile dysfunction.

Raspberries—Delicate and sensually scarlet, raspberries are considered aphrodisiac in part because of their fragility and rarity. But nutritionally, they're tiny sexual powerhouses, packed with antioxidants, manganese, potassium and magnesium.

Rose—A favorite ingredient in love potions since ancient times, Rose's sweet scent is considered a powerful tool in seducing a lover. (Legend has it that upon meeting Antony, Cleopatra had her bedroom carpeted in rose petals.) Nutritionally, rose petals are a source of vitamin C.

Rosemary—Surprisingly powerful effects come in this small package. Rosemary has an ability to increase cir-

making seal the deal
chipotle-bacon-
chocolate chippers,
pg 38

below left: hot
chocolate martini,
pg 67
below: hand rolled dark
chocolate truffles, pg 54

pistachio affogato, pg 40

below: chocolate-almond seduction cookies, pg 86

culation and aid digestion. Putting a few drops in a bath can make the skin more sensitive to touch.

Salmon—Not only is the pink fish known as one of the best sources of mood-enhancing Omega-3's, it offers calcium and vitamin A. (You knew anything that pretty on a plate had to be great for something!)

Scallops—Scallops probably first earned their aphrodisiac reputation for their voluptuous, sexy, slippery mouthfeel—a little bit of naughty on the tongue. We now know that scallops provide lean protein and iodine and may, according to the findings of a recent study, contain an amino acid that raises sexual hormone levels.

Shrimp—Shrimp offer lean protein (as in, it supplies energy all night long), iodine, Omega-3's, iron and zinc. What's not to love? *(I recommend buying wild caught shrimp, as farming practices in some countries use chemicals that can be harmful to both your health and the environment.)*

Soybeans—Soy is a sensational source of protein and, as such, can increases dopamine. It contains plant estrogens and has been helpful in relieving PMS and menopausal symptoms like vaginal dryness. There is also some evidence that soy is beneficial to prostate health.

Sparkling Wine—see Champagne

Spinach and other dark leafies—You may never have thought "spinach" and "sex" in the same sentence but dark leafy greens have got it going on in ways that will get *you* going in the bedroom. Low in calories, sans fat, spinach offers magnesium, as well as a dose of vitamins A and C. Kale, another one of the dark leafies, is off the charts in terms of vitamin A.

Strawberries—Strawberries were considered a symbol of Venus in ancient Rome. Blush red gifts of aphrodisiac goodness, they're loaded with antioxidants as well as manganese and fiber.

Tofu—*see Soybeans*

Tomatoes—Sexy, scarlet red tomatoes bring not only the color of love to the plate, but offer lycopene, beneficial to prostate health. Tomatoes are also a source of vitamins A and C.

Truffles—One for the ladies, the musky scent of truffles is said to smell almost identical to androstenone, a male pheromone. *(Truffle cologne, perhaps?)*

Vanilla—The scent of vanilla is what earns it an aphrodisiac reputation. In scientific studies, its aroma proved arousing to older men. *(Anyone for a sugar daddy?)* But beyond the power of scent, vanilla is a healthy food, containing B vitamins and traces of magnesium, manganese and zinc.

Watermelon—It was recently discovered that one of watermelon's phytonutrients, citrulline, can relax blood vessels, acting as a natural Viagra. It is also an excellent source of lycopine, beneficial to prostate health.

Whole Grains—Fiber is the friend of an aphrodisiac-laced diet. Try trading in "white foods" for as many whole grains as possible. In addition to fiber, you get beneficial B vitamins.

Wild Game—If you enjoy red meat, try wild game like buffalo, venison, wild boar, pheasant and antelope. (Farmed buffalo, venison and duck may be slightly removed from the wild but they're still great choices.) Leaner than beef and lamb, wild game meats can increases dopamine and norepinephrine production in the brain and provide sustained energy without a lot of saturated fat. Besides, serving something *wild* can make you feel like you're living on the edge!

Wine—Many experts say that a glass a day could keep the doctor away. We now know that red wine and Champagne offer powerful antioxidants. Some research has shown that the aromas of wines can replicate human pheromones. More obviously, we know that a little wine can lower inhibition and take the edge off during a romantic encounter. For more, see Chapter 8, *Don't Whine—Wine!*

Yogurt—Slathering yourself in yogurt may not make you more sexy but eating this fantastic food will provide you with protein and calcium, not to mention B vitamins, iodine and magnesium. It is also believed that a face mask of yogurt with live cultures can give the skin a certain glow.

Nutrients for Nakedness

The secret to a healthy sex life is great overall health. But nutritional science tells us that certain nutrients in particular are necessary for peak enjoyment in the games of love. I've recommended food sources for these vitamins and minerals essential for your love life. If you're interested in upping your intake of any of these nutrients with supplements rather than foods, I recommend consulting a physician to get personalized dosage recommendations.

B Vitamins—Vitamin B deficiencies only became common in the Western diet after the invention of white bread. The B's fight depression, elevate energy and mood, promote bloodflow and fight stress. We all need to make every effort possible to get our B vitamins with foods like: **whole wheat**; **brewer's yeast**; **dairy**; **beans**; **seeds** and **dark, leafy greens**.

Essential Fatty Acids—If you thought "fat" was a four-letter word, count again. Essential fatty acids not only promote muscle growth but they're needed for the production of sex hormones and can improve circulation (the better the blood pumps, the better the orgasm). Sources include: **sunflower** and **sesame oils**; **walnuts**; **peanut butter** (for linoleic acid); **salmon**; **sardines**; **anchovies** and **flax seed oil** (for Omega-3's).

Iodine—This mineral is essential to the thyroid gland. Without ample iodine, you may feel reduced sex drive and low energy. If you use iodized salt, you're already supplementing your diet but other sources include: **seafoods**; **onions**; **eggs**; **yogurt** and **pineapple**.

L-Arginine—An essential amino acid, L-Arginine increases the neurotransmitters that cause sexual arousal. It is also considered essential in obtaining sexual satisfaction, and was more recently discovered to be involved in triggering erections. It is, however, involved in the release of growth hormone, so supplements should not be taken by anyone young enough to have bones that are still growing. Food sources include: **whole wheat**; **caviar**; **chocolate**; **sesame seeds**; **oatmeal** and **popcorn**.

Magnesium—Research has proven that this mineral is absolutely essential to sex hormone production. It can also help reduce muscle soreness and cramps and can, shall we say, give your colon a call to action. (Face it, bloating is a hazard to your sex life.) To increase magnesium intake, try: **soybeans**; **meat**; **apples**; **bananas**; **figs** and **dairy products**.

Manganese—A key ingredient in eating for sexual health, manganese not only fights free radicals to prevent premature aging, but in a lab study, manganese-deficient male animals had a lack of semen and—scary—degeneration of the seminal tubules. Boys, eat your **avocado**; **nuts**; **berries**; **whole grains** and **coffee**.

Selenium—Did you know that sperm is loaded with selenium? Therefore, anyone involved with a selenium-deficient man is in trouble! Selenium is also known to boost mood and slow the aging process. Get your selenium from **onions**; **garlic**; **poultry**; **whole grains** and **mushrooms**.

Vitamin A—Some nutrients require each other to support you. Vitamin A supports vitamin E in promoting sperm production. It is also essential for a healthy thyroid. To make your vitamin A intake an A +, try: **milk**; **yams**; **pumpkin**; **eggs**; **tomatoes** and **leafy greens**.

Vitamin C—Vitamin C is a major supporter of the adrenal glands. Bluntly put, you can't have an orgasm without vitamin C. Now go eat an orange. Vitamin C is also great for the immune system and can help keep your joints limber. Besides citrus, sources of C include: **strawberries**; **raspberries**; **kale**; **bell peppers**; **papaya** and **broccoli**.

Vitamin E—Many people call it the "sex vitamin." Vitamin E is required for the production of sexual hormones and can help increase a low sperm count. It also offers antioxidant powers to keep you young and sexy. For better sex the natural way, try: **nuts**; **seeds**; **eggs**; **mangos**; **spinach** and **asparagus**.

Zinc—The "man's mineral," zinc promotes blood flow to the family jewels, aids in testosterone production and is essential for prostate health. Eat up boys: **oysters**; **pumpkin seeds**; **yogurt** and **whole grains**.

Select References

Abend, Lisa. "How Cows (Grass-Fed Only) Could Save the Planet." *Time* January 25, 2010. Web. February 20, 2010. http://www.time.com/time/magazine/article/0,9171,1953692,00.html.

Albertson, Ellen and Michael Albertson. *Temptations: igniting the pleasure and power of aphrodisiacs.* New York: Fireside, 2002.

"Dictionary of Aphrodisiac Foods." *Eat Something Sexy.* Web. January 5, 2010. http://www.eatsomethingsexy.com/aphrodisiac/index.htm.

Gaffney, Jacob. "Pop the Champagne for Heart Health." *Wine Spectator* December 9, 2009. Web. December 12, 2009. http://www.winespectator.com/webfeature/show/id/41383.

"Health Impacts." *Food & Water Watch* Web. February 10, 2010. http://www.food andwaterwatch.org/fish/fish-farming/shrimp/ health-impacts/.

Hirsch M.D., Alan R. *Scentsational Sex.* Boston: Element Books, Inc., 1998.

Lake M.D., Max. *Scents and Sesuality.* London: Futura, 1989.

Lawlis, Dr. Frank and Dr. Maggie Greenwood-Robinson. *The Brain Power Cookbook.* New York: Penguin Books, 2009.

Liebowitz M.D., Michael R. *The Chemistry of Love.* New York: Little, Brown, 1983.

McCullough, Marie. "Coffee's Health Conundrums." *The Seattle Times* July 30, 2006. Web. February 6, 2010. http://seattletimes.nwsource.com/html/health/2003 159425_healthcoffee30.html.

Mervis Watson M.D., Cynthia. *Love Potions.* Los Angeles: Tarcher/Perigee, 1993.

Nickel, Nancy L. *Nature's Aphrodisiacs.* Freedom, CA: The Crossing Press, 2001.

Pollan, Michael. *The Omnivore's Dilemma.* New York: Penguin Books, 2006.

Rolls Ph.D., Barbara. *The Volumetrics Eating Plan.* New York: Harper Collins, 2004.

Index

V

vanilla, aphrodisiac 21, 130
vinaigrette, Dijon 110
vitamin A 53, 128, 129,
   130, 134
vitamin C 34, 85, 126, 128,
   134
vitamin E 22, 86, 126, 127,
   134
vodka 52, 66

W

walnut brittle 112
watermelon 43, 130
white wine 34, 63, 95, 119

whole grains 131, 133, 134
wild game 84, 124, 131
Wilson, Chrysta 70, 103
wine 21, 34–5, 49, 63, 80,
   94, 100–1, 117–22, 124,
   131
wine and health 118–19

Y

yogurt 91, 131, 133–4
yogurt parfait 91

Z

zinc 22, 126–7, 129–30,
   134

About the Author

Amy Reiley has been recognized as a leading authority on aphrodisiac foods by publications as varied as *National Geographic* and *The London Times*. Creator of EatSomethingSexy.com, as well as author of *Fork Me, Spoon Me: the sensual cookbook,* she was the second American to earn a Master's Degree in Gastronomy from Le Cordon Bleu.

Reiley has appeared as an aphrodisiacs expert on television and radio programs from *The CBS Early Show* to NPR's *Wait Wait...Don't Tell Me!* She has also appeared on Playboy television—you'll recognize her as the one wearing clothing.

In addition to her quirky niche, Reiley is noted as an internationally published wine journalist and critic. She consults with wineries and restaurants on pairings, cocktail development and aphrodisiac-inspired events. Reiley travels, teaching and speaking on food, wine and health, with her Long-haired Chihuahua, Big and shares a home with her fiancé, on whom she tests her recipes.

She is looking forward to getting people excited about food by improving the romantic lives of home cooks everywhere!